SHEFFIELD'S WOODLAND HERITAGE

Revised Edition

Mel Jones

illustrated by
Bob Warburton

Green Tree Publications

ISBN 0 9521733 0 1

Printed in Great Britain
by
H A Burton & Co Ltd
Hanover Works, Scotland Street
Sheffield
for **Green Tree Publications**
The Grange, 4 Kirkstead Abbey Mews
Thorpe Hesley, Rotherham S61 2UZ

ii

CONTENTS

ACKNOWLEDGEMENTS

Acknowledgements are due to the staff of Sheffield Record Office for their help over a number of years; to Dan Lewis, Sheffield Recreation Department, and to Dr Ian Rotherham of the Sheffield City Ecology Unit, for their interest and for information about current management initiatives; to Brian Elliott for permission to use material from his article on the local tanning industry and in particular to reproduce Figs 39 and 40 from that article; to Mrs Avril Laurent for the loan of a photograph on which the cover and frontispiece are based; and to Worksop Public Library for providing Fig 44. We also wish to thank His Grace the Duke of Norfolk, the Trustees of the Fitzwilliam Estates and the Director of Sheffield City Libraries for permission to quote from the Arundel Castle Manuscripts and the Wentworth Woodhouse Muniments, and for Figs 11, 12, 14, 18, 19 and 20 which are reproduced from the originals in Sheffield Record Office.

Last but not least, we wish to thank Joan and Gill, our respective wives, for their patience and forbearance while the book was being written and illustrated and then revised and desk top published.

NOTE
The woodland walks which formed part of the First Edition of the book in 1989 will be issued in the near future in a separate pocket-sized booklet.

Item Hawe Parke lyeth open to Rivelin Firth...This peice is full of excellent Timber of a very great length & very Streight & many of them of a great bigness before you come to a Knott in So much that it hath been said by Travellers that they have not seene such Timber in Cristendome.

John Harrison, *An Exact and Perfect Survey and View of the Manor of Sheffield*, 1637.

The grander and more august features of nature are to be sought in regions decidedly mountainous; and are contemplated with more complete satisfaction, where the artificial creations of man have not intruded to break the harmony of the scene. But the softer graces of landscape are to be chiefly found in a district uneven but not mountainous, and may be contemplated with not less pleasure because among them are to be found some of the works of human hands. Close and well wooded valleys, with streams glittering along them, and the bare scar occasionally peeping through the foliage; hills appearing behind other hills of nearly equal altitude, some bearing fine masses of wood, and others studded with cheerful villas; views of wonderful extent, embracing variety of objects, some of which are associated with events of historical importance: - these are what the vicinity of Sheffield presents to the lovers of picturesque beauty, and which never fail to arrest the attention of the passing traveller.

Joseph Hunter, *Hallamshire*, 1819.

THE COVER ILLUSTRATION

Charcoal makers in a wood in the Sheffield area c 1890, based on an old photograph lent to the authors by Mrs A Laurent. The cabin, which is of turf over a framework of tarpaulin covered poles (the one in the doorway is clearly of birch) is typical of this area and similar ones were recorded in photographs of woods taken at Rockley near Barnsley in 1916 and in Old Shirecliffe Wood in Sheffield taken about 1890. Note the tiny cabin for the dog. The underwood and timber trees would have been felled the previous winter. The 'reserved' trees, left to grow to maturity, have been marked with white paint. Leaning against the cabin is a woodman's two-handled cross-cut saw and a series of long pointed poles which were probably used for ventilating the charcoal stacks. In the foreground is a sieve for 'riddling' the fine dust that was used to form the outer cover of the stacks, and two baskets called swills. The swills were made from strips of riven oak and were used for carrying the fine dust.

PART 1: INTRODUCTION

This book is about *ANCIENT WOODS*. The term 'ancient' when applied to woods has a precise scientific meaning. It denotes those woods that we know from documentary and landscape evidence have been in existence since at least the year 1600. In many cases it means they may be 11,000 years old! It is only since about 1650 that trees have been planted on a large scale, so any wood already in existence by 1600 may be a remnant of the so-called *wildwood* that clothed the British Isles after the melting of the ice and the thawing of the ground at the end of the last Ice Age. This does not mean that our woods today are like the wildwood. They have been managed for thousands of years, at first casually and then systematically, so that they would keep renewing themselves and so provide a never-ending supply of building materials, fuel and wood for a bewildering number of other uses. More recently they have been heavily planted and then often neglected.

Ancient woods, because of the antiquity of their woodland habitats, are of the highest natural history value. But it is a mistake to think of them only in terms of natural history. Though of natural origin, they are not wholly natural, they are semi-natural. For, as has already been pointed out, they have been managed by communities and private owners for untold generations and therefore they are as much historical monuments as castle ruins and parish churches, as much sites of industrial archaeological interest as water-powered mills and nailers' workshops.

Figure 1. A mixed party of tits feeding on an oak. Local ancient woods are full of native oak trees which support more species of insect than any other native tree.

When I visit other parts of the country and mention ancient woods in Sheffield, people's first reaction is disbelief, then surprise and finally envy. There are 6,000 acres of woodland in Sheffield Metropolitan District, a substantial proportion of which are in ancient woods. The woods that we take short cuts through, where we walk our dogs, and go into to see the displays of bluebells were also known to our medieval ancestors. But then, and indeed until the end of the

1

nineteenth century, they were all working woods. Our ancestors lived in a 'Wood Age' and the former significance of the woods within or near which they lived and from which they obtained many of their basic resources, remains with us, passed down to us by our predecessors in family names and the names of the places in which we live.

Figure 2. Ancient woods are historic monuments. *The woods we take short cuts through, where we walk our dogs, and go into to see the displays of bluebells, were also known to our medieval ancestors. This drawing is based on a photograph taken in Bowden Housteads Wood which lies between Darnall, the Manor and Handsworth, and is divided into two by the Parkway. The wood was mentioned in a document written in 1332.*

Surviving medieval documents as well as modern telephone directories for the Sheffield area are full of surnames suggesting a well-wooded environment. There are names meaning wood such as Greaves, Firth, Hirst, Shaw, Storrs, Ashirst, Haslehurst, and, of course, Wood itself; then there are surnames derived from the names of trees such as Ash, Birks, Birch, Oakes, Maples, and Hollings; names meaning woodland clearing like Lee, Thwaites, and Royds; and names from woodland occupations including Forster, Barker, Tanner, Woodman, and Woodward.

Ten minutes with a local map is enough to confirm suspicions that this area was once a well-wooded one. There are still some substantial woods, and woodland fragments are widely distributed. Moreover, the names of villages and suburbs also point to a once wooded landscape. Place-names of Old English (Saxon) origin containing the elements -ley and -field, which mean woodland clearing, are everywhere: Sheffield, Bradfield, Ecclesfield, Holmesfield, Heeley, Loxley, Mortomley, Tinsley, Gleadless, and Norton Lees. Also present but less common are Old Norse names meaning wood such as Lound and Storrs, and woodland clearing (-thwaite) as at Butterthwaite.

But what is known of the extensive woods that have for so long clothed the Sheffield area and which still make it such a pleasant place in which to live and work? How natural or artificial are they? Who owned them in the past? How were they managed? Have they always looked like they do today? Until recently little had been written about woods in general and next to nothing about local woods, and the questions posed above had not even been asked, let alone answered. This is rather surprising in view of the undoubted importance of woods in the local economy until relatively recently.

One reason for the awakening interest in ancient woods is the realisation that they are fast disappearing or are being changed out of all recognition. Of the million and a quarter acres of ancient broadleaved woodland that had survived in Britain until 1945, 30 per cent (375,000 acres) have since been converted into coniferous plantations, and 100,000 acres have been cleared altogether. In the Sheffield area, although many ancient woods have survived there have been some important losses. Shirecliffe Park Wood, which Joseph Hunter in 1819 said 'so beautifully clothes with a forest vesture the ground declining to the River Don' finally disappeared in the 1926 strike, and Tinsley Park which in the mid-seventeenth century was a 400 acre woodland now covers no more than a few acres. Greno Wood and Hall Wood have been largely coniferised, and this process has destroyed their ground flora and impoverished them as wildlife habitats. In Gillfield Wood at Totley the native tree and shrub species have been largely replaced by American red oak, sycamore and larch. Other woods have been adversely affected by mining activity and road and rail developments.

Despite these losses and changes - and this may come as much as a surprise to residents as it does to visitors - Sheffield contains at least 35 ancient woods (see Figure 3), one of which is a Site of Special Scientific Interest (SSSI). Sheffield is probably the best wooded city in Britain.

But all is not well. Vandalism and neglect are taking their toll in the more accessible woods and there are development pressures on some woods. The complex communities of native trees, shrubs, herbs, grasses and sedges of the ancient woods, their associated animal life, largely undisturbed soils, and their historical features, once destroyed, can never be recreated. These irreplaceable assets will at best be sadly depleted and at worst prodigally squandered unless a sympathetic, long-term management policy is vigorously pursued. Thankfully, there are moves in the right direction, but there is still much that needs to be done. This issue is taken up again in Part 5.

This small book is a modest attempt to make the natural and economic history of our local ancient woods more widely known and to explain some of their more obvious present-day features. Part 2 is concerned with the historical development of Sheffield's woods and the ways in which they were managed in the past. This is followed in Part 3 by a look at some of the many crafts and industries that were once dependent on timber and wood from the local woodlands. Part 4 considers the clues that are present in our woods today that tell us about their origins and their history. Finally, in Part 5, the future of Sheffield's woods is considered.

Figure 3. Known ancient woods in Sheffield. Research amongst documents dating from the fourteenth to the twentieth century shows that the sites located and named on the map opposite have been continuously occupied by woodland for at least the last four centuries. The woods vary in quality. In some cases their character has been radically altered by the decline in traditional management, by neglect, by vandalism, by mining activity, by the planting of exotics and conifers, and by transport developments.

1	*Reeley Wood*	*18*	*Low Spring*
2	*Birkin Royd*	*19*	*Little Matlock Wood*
3	*Blackbrook Wood*	*20*	*Loxley Common*
4	*Bowden Housteads Wood*	*21*	*Park Bank Wood*
5	*Brushes*	*22*	*Parkin Wood*
6	*Buck Wood*	*23*	*Prior Royd*
7	*Carr Wood*	*24*	*Rollestone Wood*
8	*Chancet Wood*	*25*	*Scraith Wood*
9	*Clough or Ladies Clough Wood*	*26*	*Smith's Wood*
10	*Ecclesall Woods*	*27*	*Smithy Wood*
11	*Gillfield Wood*	*28*	*Snaithing Spring*
12	*Great Roe Wood*	*29*	*Tinsley Park (remnant)*
13	*Greno Wood*	*30*	*Ladies Spring Wood (SSSI)*
14	*Hall Wood*	*31*	*West Wood*
15	*Hesley Wood*	*32*	*Wheata Wood*
16	*Hutcliffe Wood*	*33*	*Wilson Spring*
17	*Lee Shroggs Wood*	*34*	*Wincobank Wood*
		35	*Woolley Wood*

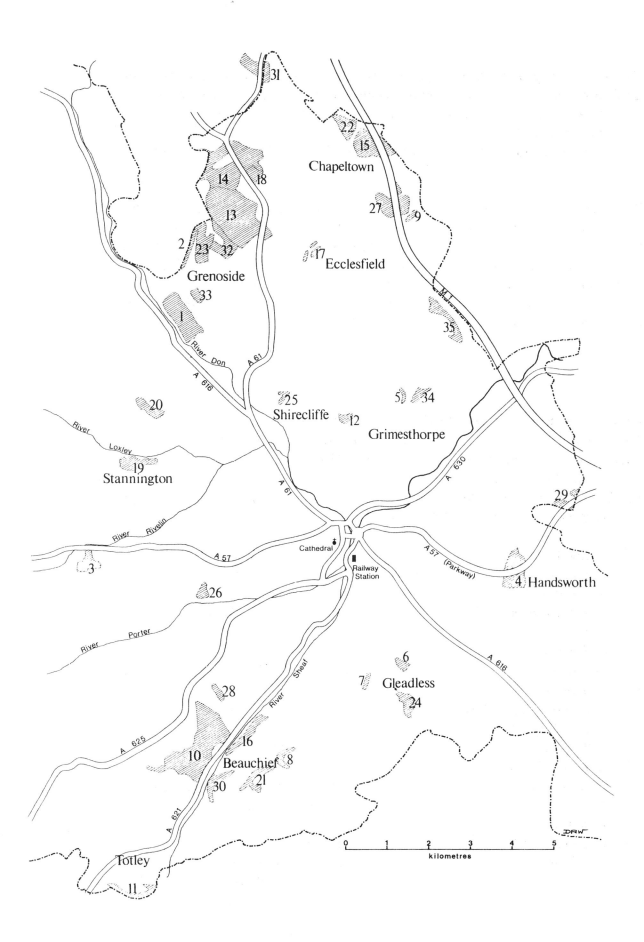

31

22
15
Chapeltown

14 18

27 9

2 23 32
13

Grenoside
33
17 Ecclesfield
1

River Don
A 61
A 616

M1
35

20
River Loxley
19
Stannington

25
Shirecliffe
12

5 34

Grimesthorpe

A 630
29

River Rivelin
A 61

A 57
Cathedral

Railway
Station

A 57 (Parkway)
4 Handsworth

3

26
River Porter

River Sheaf

6
7 Gleadless
24

A 616

A 625

28

16
10
Beauchief 8
30 21

A 621

0   1   2   3   4   5
kilometres

Totley

11

DRW

5

PART 2: THE ORIGINS AND HISTORY OF SHEFFIELD'S WOODS

The Wildwood

The woodland history of the British Isles in general and of the Sheffield region in particular began about 13,000 years ago (c.11,000 B.C.), when the last glaciers and ice sheets of the Ice Age melted, frozen ground thawed and climatic conditions improved to the point where trees could move in again from those parts of Western Europe that had lain beyond the grip of ice and freezing conditions.

Seeds borne on the wind or spread in the droppings of birds and mammals enabled a wave of colonisation to make its way across the British Isles from the south-east. The progress of the colonisation has been reconstructed by using the pollen grains produced by trees, and which are very resistent to decay, that accumulated in bogs, lakes and ponds. Microscopic analysis enables the pollen of one species of tree to be distinguished from that of another. Using this evidence, scientists have been able to show that the first trees to colonise post-glacial Britain were arctic trees such as aspen, birch and willow, the last two of which are still usually the first trees to grow on bare ground. Later came pine and hazel, then alder and oak. Later still came elm and lime and finally ash, holly, hornbeam and maple.The later trees found it more difficult to spread because the bare ground had already been occupied by the early colonisers. There then followed a long period of adjustment as particular species consolidated their dominance in particular localities, failed to gain a foothold in others or were pushed out by other, invasive, species.

Figure 4. The Wildwood. *No one knows what the Wildwood looked like. There must have been many very old, very large trees and, where these had crashed down, thickets of young growth. There must also have been many dead trees: standing, leaning against neighbours and lying on the woodland floor in various stages of decomposition. Pollen analysis suggests there were permanent glades of various sizes scattered throughout the Wildwood which would have been grazed and kept treeless by wild cattle and deer.*

By about 4,000 B.C. the wildwood, a term coined by the Cambridge ecologist, Oliver Rackham, to describe Britain's woods before they were interfered with by humans, was fully developed. By that time particular parts of the country, as revealed by pollen analysis, were dominated by particular trees. Although there must have been much local variation, the general picture seems to have been as follows. The extreme north of Scotland was still tundra - like northern Norway and Sweden today - and virtually treeless. Most of the north-western Highlands of Scotland were covered in birch forests while the eastern Highlands were dominated by pine. The rest of Scotland, northern England, the north midlands, the south-west and most of Wales were covered by forests dominated by oak and hazel. Hazel and elm occupied south-west Wales and most of Cornwall. The rest of England was covered by woods in which lime was the dominant tree.

The picture is summarised in Figure 5 and what is interesting and what makes the Sheffield region such a fascinating one for woodlands is that Sheffield lies very close to the boundary between the oak-hazel province and the lime dominated province. And this difference is still evident in our modern woodlands. Woods in the Bradfield area are not dissimilar to woods found in the Lake District, while those just to the south-east of the city are not unlike woods in Suffolk or Kent. The native small-leaved lime (in Latin *Tilia cordata*) is still found 'growing wild' in relatively large numbers in Anston Stones Wood and King's Wood in the south-eastern part of Rotherham and in a wood in the Moss valley just beyond the southern boundary of Sheffield, but it is virtually unknown within Sheffield's boundaries. On the other hand, despite much planting, oak is still one of the commonest trees in Sheffield and old records show that it dominated many of the city's woods in the past.

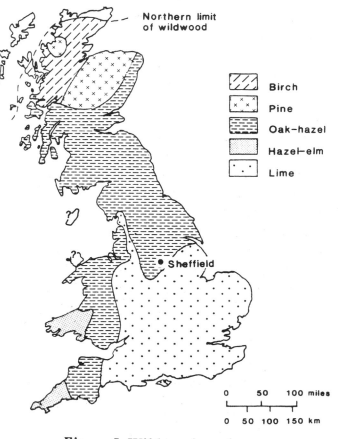

Figure 5. Wildwood provinces.

The clearance of the Wildwood

Deliberate clearance of the wildwood by humans has been taking place for the last 6,000 years, first by the pastoralist Neolithic peoples who entered our region about 4,000 B.C., and then by the successive expansion of agricultural settlement and land use in the Bronze Age (1,900 - 500 B.C.), Iron Age (500 B.C. - 50 A.D., the Roman period (50 - 450 A.D.), and in the succeeding Dark Ages during which time Anglo-Saxon and Scandinavian colonists settled widely. Woodland clearance continued throughout the Middle Ages and into the modern period, at first for agricultural land as before but later accompanied on a large scale by mining activity and urban and industrial expansion.

7

The prehistoric settlers in the Sheffield region have left little direct evidence of their woodland clearance activity though the finds of stone and metal axes and other implements, hut circles, burial mounds and other earthworks, and the increasing number of settlement sites that are being located using aerial photographs taken during periods of drought when they show up clearly as cropmarks, all indicate a long occupation of the region that must have been accompanied by much woodland destruction by axe and by grazing by domesticated animals.

It was the Anglo-Saxon, Scandinavian and medieval occupants of the region who left behind, through the names they gave to fields, farms and villages, widespread evidence of a countryside once covered by and then gradually cleared of woodland. Some of these names tell us about the composition of the wildwood that was being cleared. To the south-east of Sheffield just inside Nottinghamshire is the village of Carlton in Lindrick. Lindrick is a word of Anglo-Saxon origin meaning 'lime wood'. Agden in Bradfield is also a Saxon name and means 'oak valley'.

The most widespread of these early place-names are those that mean woodland clearing. Many must indicate large clearings that had existed for many generations before the Anglo-Saxons or Scandinavians entered the region and they were merely renaming them in their own language, but they must have been greatly enlarged and others created as first Saxon and then Scandinavian colonisation took place. Two Old English (Anglo-Saxon) place-name elements that mean clearing that are widespread in the Sheffield region are -ley and -field. The -ley element helps to make up names like Heeley (high clearing), Longley (long clearing), Hartley (clearing frequented by stags), Totley (clearing of Tota's people), Walkley (Walca's clearing), and Norton Lees (clearing at Norton). The -field element which should be interpreted more like the Afrikaans veldt than our modern word field, gives us names like Sheffield (treeless countryside near the River Sheaf), Bradfield (broad stretch of open countryside) and Ecclesfield (open countryside in which stood a British (Celtic) church). The Old Norse (Scandinavian) equivalent of -field was -thwaite as in Butterthwaite at Ecclesfield (clearing with rich pasture).

Other significant local early names indicating settlement in a well wooded countryside are -royd as in Prior Royd at Ecclesfield, which is Old English and again means clearing, storth as in Storrs at Stannington which is Old Norse for wood, and -lund as in Lound Side at Chapeltown which is also Old Norse and means a small wood or grove. Names like Woodseats as in Norton Woodseats and Woodhouse as in Wentworth Woodhouse are medieval and indicate an offshoot settlement in the woods surrounding the original settlement.

The map showing village, hamlet and farm names (including those now part of the main urban areas) in South Yorkshire indicating woodland and woodland clearing (Figure 6) suggests that originally the wildwood was almost continuous in the western half of the county in what are now Sheffield and Barnsley Metropolitan Districts, whereas in the eastern half large areas were cleared so early or were never thickly wooded so that woodland and woodland clearance names are uncommon. This east-west contrast in South Yorkshire is taken up again in the next section.

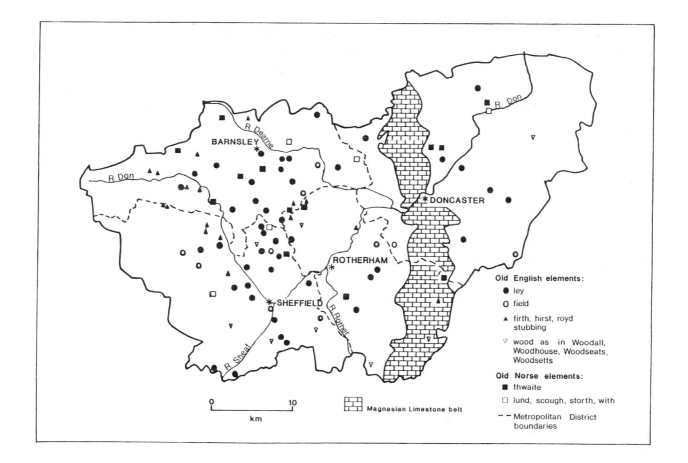

Figure 6. Old English and Old Norse place-names in South Yorkshire indicating woodland and woodland clearance.

Woodland at the time of the Domesday survey

The amount of woodland more or less permanently cleared in the 6,000 years between the entry of Neolithic peoples to the British Isles and King William's nation-wide survey of his kingdom in 1086 must have varied a great deal from district to district and region to region. What is increasingly clear is that in general the woodland cover had been drastically reduced by Norman times and the countryside was not covered by the boundless wildwood of people's imagination. In many areas what we in the late twentieth century think of as the typical English countryside of hedged or walled fields, winding lanes, isolated farms, hamlets and villages and scattered woods was already in existence and had been for centuries.

Oliver Rackham, in *The History of the Countryside* (1986), calculates that the Domesday survey covered 27 million acres of land of which 4.1 million were wooded, that is 15 per cent of the surveyed area. His figure for the West Riding of Yorkshire is 16 per cent. My own calculation for South Yorkshire is just under 13 per cent. By way of comparison woods today, including plantations, cover just over six per cent of the county. What this all means is that in the eleventh century the country generally and our local area in particular were relatively sparsely wooded even

9

by twentieth century standards, but regionally, and as we shall see, locally, there were great variations.

Before looking at the types and distribution of woods in the Sheffield area in the eleventh century it is helpful to look at a typical South Yorkshire Domesday woodland entry and to be aware of the difficulties of interpretation. The entries for the manors of Hallam, Ecclesfield, Holdworth, Ughill, Worrall and Wadsley which together more or less coincide with the present Metropolitan District of Sheffield are as follows:

Hallam
wood pasture 4 leagues long and 4 wide

Ecclesfield
wood pasture 1 league and a half long and the same wide

Holdworth
wood pasture 1 league long and 1 wide

Ughill, Worrall and Wadsley
wood pasture 1 league long and 1 wide

Disregarding the precise meaning of the term 'wood pasture' for the moment, it can be seen that the major problem is to convert the Domesday length and breadth measurements into modern areal units. It is generally assumed that a Domesday league was twelve furlongs or a mile and a half. This assumption would give, of course, the dimensions of woodlands that were perfectly square or rectangular, and this was never the case in reality. Moreover, in many cases the linear dimensions must have been arrived at by lumping together two or more woods. To overcome these problems what is called a 'form factor' is used. This is a statistic used to compensate for the oversimplification of the Domesday entries. After comparing Domesday entries with medieval woods of known size which are known not to have changed in the intervening period, Oliver Rackham suggests a form factor of 0.7, i.e. if you multipy the length by the breadth, you must then assume that the woodland area would be about 70 per cent of the figure arrived at. Applying this to Domesday Sheffield would give:

For Hallam

4 leagues x 4 leagues
= 6 x 6 miles = 36 square miles
= 23,040 acres x 0.7
= 16,128 acres

For Ecclesfield

1.5 leagues x 1.5 leagues
= 2.25 x 2.25 miles = 5.06 square miles

10

= 3,240 acres x 0.7
= 2,268 acres

For Holdworth

1 league x 1 league
= 1.5 x 1.5 miles = 2.25 square miles
= 1,440 acres x 0.7
= 1,008 acres

For Ughill,Worrall and Wadsley

1 league x 1 league
= 1.5 x 1.5 miles = 2.25 square miles
= 1,440 acres x 0.7
= 1,008 acres

This gives a total Domesday woodland area for what is now Sheffield Metropolitan District of 20,412 acres. This represents 22.5 per cent of the land area. At the present time woods and plantations cover about 6,000 acres or about 6.6 per cent of the land area.

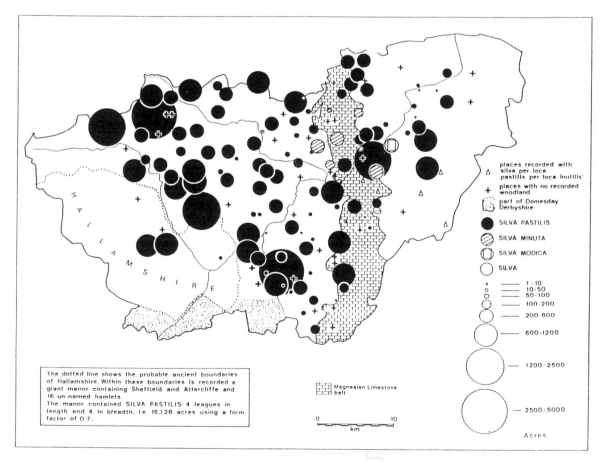

Figure 7. Woodland in South Yorkshire at Domesday.

11

Bearing in mind the way that Domesday woodland areas are calculated for South Yorkshire we can now turn to Figure 7 which shows the distribution and types of woodland in the county in 1086. With the exception of the giant manor of Hallam, places with woods are shown by circles varying in size according to the extent of the woodland. There are noticeable variations in the distribution of woodland. In the west in what is now Sheffield, Barnsley and the western half of Rotherham Metropolitan Districts, woodland was relatively extensive with a substantial number of communities having more than 1000 acres of wood.

In contrast, in the eastern part of the county, in what is now the eastern part of Rotherham Metropolitan District and the whole of Doncaster Metropolitan District, the picture was very different. In those areas woodland was more scattered, amounts in individual communities were much smaller than in the west and in nineteen places no woodland was recorded at all. This suggests early clearance and continuous occupation and cultivation by a relatively dense population for thousands of years. It can be seen that within this part of the county is a belt of Magnesian Limestone country which has long been regarded as the most fertile and attractive area for early settlement in South Yorkshire. This is borne out by the small amount of woodland at Domesday and by the almost total absence of woodland clearance names amongst the villages there. This last point suggests that it was already an area with little woodland when the Saxon and Scandinavian settlers, from whom most of our village names are derived, arrived in the area.

The types of woodland in South Yorkshire at Domesday also suggest a shortage of woodland in the east of the county and a relative abundance in the west including the whole of the Sheffield area.

When woods were widespread and populations sparse and scattered they would have been exploited for their trees and also as pastures for cattle, pigs and sheep. Woods used in this way are referred to as **wood pasture**. As populations grew, and demands on the timber increased, and pressure from grazing animals prevented regeneration, woods became scarce and valuable resources and had to be fenced to prevent animals entering them. At the same time a type of management which gave a continuous and self-renewing supply of trees had to be introduced. This was achieved by cutting the trees to ground level and allowing them to grow up again. This is called **coppicing**.

Turning to Figure 7 again, the key shows that Domesday woodland in the county was described in four different ways: *silva, silva modica, silva minuta and silva pastilis. Silva* is simply woodland; the meaning of *silva modica* is not clear; *silva minuta* is coppice; and *silva pastilis* is wood pasture. Of the 111 places in which woodland was recorded in South Yorkshire, seven had coppice woods and 102 had wood pastures. All seven areas of coppice wood were in the eastern half of the county with five in the Magnesian Limestone belt, underlining the view that it was an area of dense population. On the other hand, although wood pasture was found in all parts of the county it was very extensive and the only type of woodland found in the west including the whole of the Sheffield area.

To sum up, more than one-fifth of the Sheffield area at Domesday was covered by woodland. This woodland was so extensive and the population so small and scattered that animals were allowed to graze in the woods.

Woodland management from the Middle Ages to the nineteenth century

In the centuries following the Domesday survey, although the wood pasture tradition in the area continued to be strong, especially on wooded commons and in deer parks, coppice management gradually became the norm in order to conserve wood supplies which were becoming depleted as the population grew and more and more woodland was cleared for agriculture. Having said that, however, evidence available at the present time suggests that coppice management, which had probably been practised outside and within wood pastures on a casual basis since Neolithic times, did not replace wood pasture in the Sheffield area as the dominant form of woodland management until a comparatively late date.

For example, in a deed dated 1161, the monks of Ecclesfield Priory were given the right to pasture their flocks every year from January to Easter in a large wood stretching from Birley Edge down to the Don (Beeley Wood is a remnant of this large wood and part of it is still called Priory Wood). This suggests a wood pasture regime, for, as we shall see later, coppicing and flocks of grazing animals are incompatible. Nearly 200 years later in 1332, in a document written following the death of Thomas de Furnival, the lord of the Manor of Sheffield, eleven localities were listed under the heading of pastures in woods, moors and commons, including Greno Wood, Beeley Wood and Bowden Housteads Wood, all of which 300 years later were coppice woods in which animals were unwelcome.

In coppice management the timing and manner of felling were strictly controlled and grazing animals were only allowed into the woods when the trees were well enough grown that flocks would not destroy them by devouring young growth. In accordance with an overall plan most of the trees in a particular wood, or part of a wood if it were large, would be cut close to the ground and from the stump or **stool** (see Figure 8) sprang a number of **poles** (hence the name

Figure 8. **Coppice.** *From left to right: a newly coppiced stool; stool coppiced last winter; three-year old coppice growth; neglected coppice.*

spring wood). The poles were known as **coppice, underwood** or just **wood**. They were cut regularly, the period of growth before being cut again - called the **coppice cycle** - varying from just a few years in the case of hazel for basket and hurdle making to 25 years or more if the main products were pit props.

There is no reason why a stool should not supply a crop of underwood for many centuries. This form of management, therefore, conserved woods and if properly managed and protected they became self-renewing resources and inexhaustible sources of wood.

In the Sheffield area, the form of coppice management called **coppice with standards** had emerged as the norm by the late Middle Ages. In woods managed in this way, among the coppice growth young trees were selected to become timber trees and therefore were not coppiced. These were the standards and they remained through a number of coppice cycles, depending on the demand for timber, and were felled as the market required. Whereas the underwood, though predominantly of oak, was mixed (and in South Yorkshire included ash, maple, hawthorn, crab apple, birch, hazel, willow, rowan, and, more rarely, lime and wild service), the standards were overwhelmingly of oak, though ash and alder were locally important. When young the timber trees were called **wavers**. When they had grown through two coppice cycles they were referred to locally as **black barks**. They were then 40-50 years old. Older timber trees were known as **lordings**. A diagrammatic representation of a coppice with standards is shown in Figure 9.

Figure 9. A diagrammatic representation of a wood managed as a coppice with standards.
On the left is a compartment in which the underwood has been cut recently and there is little new growth. In the compartment on the right the underwood is several years old and has sprung from the stools to a height of five or six feet. Among the underwood are five standards: two mature trees that have grown through several coppice cycles and three younger trees (wavers). The wood is bounded on the left by a bank and ditch surmounted by a hedge. On the woodbank is a pollard, a tree coppiced about six feet above ground so that the growth is beyond the reach of browsing animals in the adjacent field.

One of the earliest surviving records of coppice with standards management in the Sheffield area is a lease written in Latin and dated 1421. The lease concerns a farm at Norton and contains a number of clauses concerning charcoal burning and the right to cut underwood and timber. The document refers to the coppices on the farm as **le Spryng bosci**, an interesting mixture of French, English and Latin, and to the timber by the usual Latin word of **maerimium**. Specific woods were not named.

Two other medieval records of coppice with standards that do mention specific woods have survived. The first, dated 1462 and written in English, refers to a number of localities in Norton parish thus: '...all the wood growing in Rowhawe, Gilleclose, herdyng wood, Whistenhalker, Jacfield, Colynfield and Whitefield...'. Herdyng Wood is the old name for Rollestone Wood which still stands in the middle of the Gleadless Valley housing estate. The document records that John Cotes and John Parker had been granted permission by William Chaworth, knight and lord of Norton,'...to fell...cole (i.e. to make into charcoal) and carye the said Woddes...' preserving for the owner '...sufficiaunt Wayvers after the custom of the contre...'. The mention of wavers, the young timber trees, shows that the woods in question were coppices with standards. Wavers are also mentioned in the second document which refers to Hutcliff Wood in the Sheaf valley at Abbeydale and was written in 1496. The wood at that time was the property of Beauchief Abbey and the document records that '...the abbot of Beucheff...' had granted permission '...to cooll (i.e. to make into charcoal) ii certen wodds that is to say hudclyff and the brood medowe Abutt...', the woods to be left '...weyverd workmonlyke...'.

By the end of the sixteenth century coppicing was general. In an undated document written for the 7th Earl of Shrewsbury, the major landowner in Sheffield who succeeded to the title in 1590 and died in 1616, eleven woods still in existence in Sheffield were listed, and they were all listed as spring woods. The woods were Woolley Wood, Hall Wood, Greno Wood, Wilson Spring, Beeley Wood, West Wood, Hesley Wood, Smithy Wood, Bowden Housteads Wood, Wincobank Wood and Roe Wood. Altogether the list gave the names of 49 coppice woods in Sheffield and Rotherham. An extract from the list is shown in Figure 10.

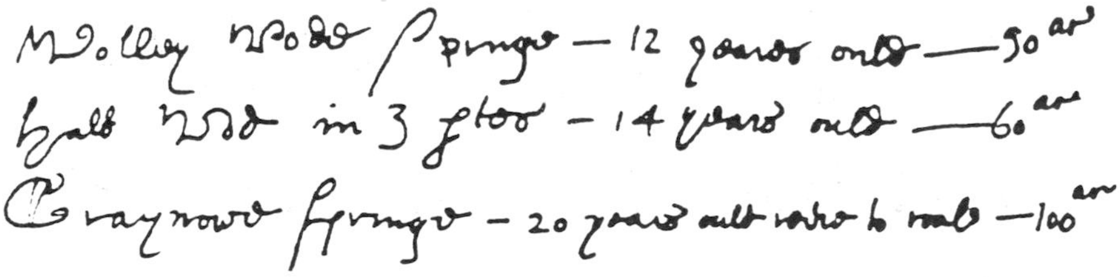

Figure 10. Extract from a document now in Lambeth Palace Library, London, which was written between 1590-1616 for the 7th Earl of Shrewsbury. It listed his spring woods in Yorkshire. In the extract the woods named are Woolley Wood, Hall Wood and Greno Wood.

John Harrison in his '...*exact and perfect Survey & View of the Mannor of Sheffield...*' that he completed for the Earl of Arundel and Surrey in 1637 listed 36 separate spring woods in which the underwood varied in age from four years to 40. Although Harrison did not mention timber trees in the spring woods he named and described, it is clear from other near contemporary documents that the woods on the Arundel estate in Sheffield and Rotherham and on the neighbouring Wentworth estate were nearly all coppices with standards.

Various aspects of coppice with standards management in South Yorkshire are well illustrated in two schemes preserved in the Wentworth Woodhouse archives. These schemes were devised by Thomas Wentworth, 1st Marquis of Rockingham, who inherited the Wentworth estates in 1723. In what is called his Rent Roll, but what is also a record of his building and other estate activities, he wrote out in his own hand in 1727 what he called 'A Scheme for making a yearly considerable Profit of Spring Woods in Yorkshire', and in 1749 what he described as 'A Scheme for a Regular Fall of Wood for 21 years...'. In the 1749 scheme a 21 year cycle was used so that the woods coppiced in 1749 would be cut again in 1771. This meant that the Marquis' 876 acres of woodland in South Yorkshire would produce a regular crop of 40 acres of underwood a year for 21 years at which point the crop in the first wood to be cut, would be ready to be cut again. Two of the woods in the scheme, West Wood (at High Green) and Tinsley Park, were so extensive that they were divided into separate compartments that were coppiced at different times. The Marquis was very specific about the timber trees: there were to be five reserves (mature timber trees called black barks) and 70 wavers (sapling timber trees) per acre. The full scheme is shown in Figure 11.

The practice of compartmenting large coppice woods is graphically shown in a series of detailed maps produced by the Duke of Norfolk's woodward in 1810 and which can be seen in the Sheffield Record Office. Besides showing the compartments into which the large woods were divided, each map gives the dates of the last fall and the numbers of reserves and wavers preserved in each compartment. One of these maps showing Hall Wood at High Green, a well documented wood that had hardly changed its shape at all in the almost two centuries since Harrison's 1637 survey, is reproduced as Figure 12.

Coppice woods were looked after by woodwards or coppice keepers who kept a vigilant lookout for trespassers and thieves. The proceedings of local manorial courts and woodwards' accounts are full of instances of waiting for and catching offenders, of accusations of theft and trespass, of appearances in court, of fines, and of payments to woodwards' helpers for tracking down suspects and repossessing stolen wood, timber and bark.

The illegal felling and carrying away of underwood and timber were the most widely reported offences. For example, in 1564 William Dungworth was fined twelvepence for felling and carrying away wood in the Earl of Shrewsbury's Wincobank Wood and in the same year Thomas Beaumont was similarly fined for felling and taking away two loads of wood from 'le Firth of Revelinge'. Most cases were of small thefts but occasionally large thefts were reported. In 1731, for example, Mrs Letitia Pegge brought an action against Anthony Fox for carrying away 20 oak trees and 104 cartloads of wood from Park Bank Wood on the Beauchief estate.

From time to time there were eruptions of widespread theft and these led to concerted action. Towards the end of the second decade of the eighteenth century the level of thefts from the Duke of Norfolk's woods was such that Abraham Ibbotson, the Duke's woodward in Sheffield, was

A Scheme for a Regular Fall of Wood for 21 Years to come from the Year 1749 of about 42 Acres a Year the Coppice Woods in Yorkshire amounting to about nine Hundred Acres, in which calculation Scholes Wood, all timber Trees & Woods in the Park at Wentworth are not included, nor the Woods in Northamptonshire, particularly Withmail Park of 100 Acres nor a Wood of about 30 Acres at Yesthrop Park which was felled Anno 1726 - Reserves to be at least 5 Black Barks & 70 Wavers - Philip Wood 2 Acres 2 Roods being Holted is not included nor the Wood by the Pyramide.

	Acres
Tinsley Park at Nine Falls for the Years 1749, 1750, 1751, 1753, 1754, 1755, 1756 & 1757	350
Anno 1758 Bassingthorp Spring	37
Anno 1759 Great Thorncliffe	37
Anno 1760 Harley Spring 18A Luke Spring 8 - 2 Goss Wood 8 Acres Bank Spring 4 Acres	totall 38 - 2
Anno 1761 Giles Wood 24 Acres King's Wood 11 Normandale Springs 5 Bolderfall 2A 2R	totall 42 - 2

Anno 1762 Tindle Brig Spring 4A 2R Wadsworth Spring 1 - 2R
     Westfield Ing Spring 3 Acres Simon Wood 25 - 2R
     Birkfield Spring 7A - 2R Coney Garth Spring 2A - 2R
	totall 43 - 2

1763 Law Wood - 40 Acres	40 - 0

1764 Street Wood - 13 Rowing Spring 4A - 2R
      Littlewood Ing Spg 5 Acres 2 Roods Thorncliff
      Bottoms 5A Blackmoor Bottoms 1A Longland Spring
      & Longley Bottoms 5A Little Thorncliffe 3
	totall 37 - 0

1765, 1766, 1767 upper Linthwait 5A - 2R Golden being three Years Fall Smithys 4 Rainbergh 115	totall 124 - 2
38 acres Per Annum	
Anno 1768, 1769 & 1770 Westwood exclusive of all Wasts being a Fall of 42 Acres Per each Year & so begin the Circle again excluding all wast to fall	126 - 2 876

N.B. no Spinneys of Plantations in Wentworth Park & Demesnes are Included - There are also some little Reins & Spinneys up and down not taken notice of - also hedge Rows A Wood at Yesthorpe Park 30 Acres

Figure 11. The Marquis of Rockingham's 1749 coppice wood scheme. Source: WWM 1273.

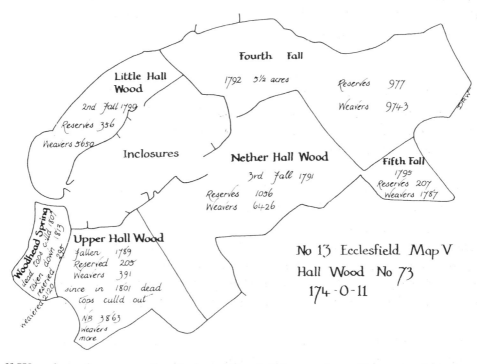

Figure 12. Hall Wood as shown on the Duke of Norfolk's woodward's map of 1810.

granted a warrant by the justices of the peace instructing local constables to '...make diligent search...in the most suspitious houses...' and to bring suspects before the magistrates. The inclusion in the warrant, which is given in full in Figure 13, of the phrases 'All Excuses & Delays Sett apart' and 'Faile not at your perrills' indicates the seriousness of the situation. Ibbotson wrote up in his accounts in the following year a claim for 3s for '...2 days spent in searching Ecclesfield p'ish for wood cutt down in Roe Wood'. In the same year he paid the constable of Nether Hallam five shillings for reporting fourteen people to the justices of the peace for stealing birch twigs, and informers and witnesses were paid £1-5-0.

There were particularly sensitive times of the year in the woods. In autumn when berries and nuts were ripe, and in winter, when firewood and food supplies were low, thefts were particularly common. The practice of collecting hazel nuts in local woods caused widespread damage to wood boundaries and the underwood and prompted the Pegges of Beauchief in 1809 and the

> To all Constables within the West Riding of the County of Yorke whom it may concerne Especially to ye Constables within ye sev'll mannors of ye most Noble Lord Thomas Duke of Norfolk Earle Marshall
>
> Whereas Complaint hath been made to us that Great destruction hath been of Late & Frequently is made in ye woods growing in ye sev'all mannors Lordshipps & Libties of ye said Thomas Duke of Norfolk by being cutt downe & carried away by Some Idle Disorderly persons and before Any Warrent can be had from any Justice of ye Peace to search for ye wood so cutt downe & destroyed ye parties offending convey ye same to such obscure places or otherwise dispose of ye Same That there Can nothing be found Against them for their conviction.
>
> These are therefore in his Maties name strictly to Charge and Command you & Evy of You (All Excuses & Delays Sett apart) that at what times and Seasons when and as often as Abraham Ibbotson of Sheffield Gent shall Resort unto yu or any of you with this our precept that by vertue hereof you make diligent Search according to Law in the most suspitious houses outhouses and other places within any of your Limmitts or Libties of all & Evy such person or persons whome you shall Justly Suspect or be informed to have done ye same and where you find any such wood that you secure the same & bring such suspected persons before us or Some other of his Maties Justices of ye peace for ye sd Riding to answer ye premises & be examined Concerning ye same hereof faile not at your perrills This Precept or warrent Dormant to Continue in full force for one Compleat year next ensuing ye date hereof & no longer Given under our hands & seald ye fifteenth day of October An. dom 1718
>
> Signed and sealed by W Jessop and J Bradshaw

Figure 13. Warrant issued by the Justices of the Peace in 1718 at the request of Abraham Ibbotson, the Duke of Norfolk's woodward. Source: ACM 541.

18

Duke of Norfolk in 1812 to post warning notices around their estate and woodland boundaries. The Beauchief notice is shown in Figure 14.

Trespass, as a prelude to theft or in the course of taking short cuts was also a common offence. This was accomplished by making gaps in hedges or climbing walls and the damage thus caused, that could lead to animals browsing among the coppice, was of great concern to woodwards. In 1441 William de Housley was fined sixpence for trespassing in Greno Wood and breaking down the hedge. On 20 May 1720 Joseph Shepherd and his wife were paid two shillings for '...watching to see who breaks ye Gapp open at ye upper side of Shertley Park (Shirecliffe Park Wood)'. The Duke of Norfolk's woodward annotated his entry in the account book to the effect that '...M. Bamforth Pull'd it open'. Six years later the Duke's woodward paid Richard Wainwright three shillings for waiting for, watching and catching Robert Rawson, a carrier,'...who was supposed to break ye old hedge at Shirecliffe Park Wood'.

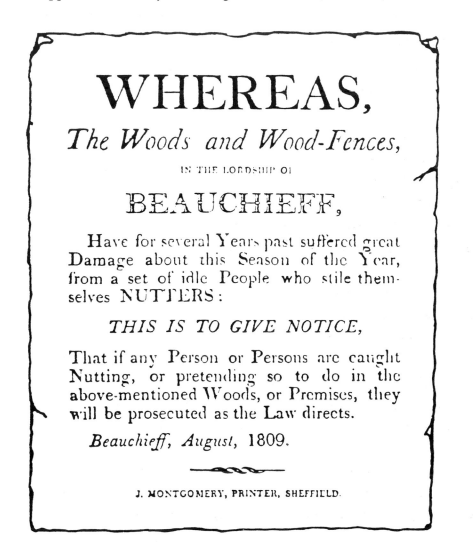

Figure 14. Warning to hazel nut gatherers, Beauchief estate, 1809. Source: BM 33-21.

19

When the coppice was well grown, tenants' animals were allowed access to the woods on payment of a due. For example, Joseph Ashmore, who was woodward to the Duke of Norfolk in the early 1700s, charged himself two shillings in 1710 for 'My Mare & fole in Wooley Woods this Spring a month it's old Cutt'. This practice was called **herbage** or **agistment**.

Sometimes it was necessary to remind the local population that a coppice cycle had just been completed, that the new coppice was at a critical stage in its growth, and that animals should not be allowed to enter the woods. In this connection the vicar of Ecclesfield was paid twopence in 1718 for giving notice to tenants and freeholders, presumably at a Sunday service, to '...take care that their cattle do no longer Continue to Graise in Greno Wood for Spoyling ye young sprouts'.

In spite of such precautions animals were always likely to stray into woods from neighbouring pastures and commons and this was guarded against by building and keeping in good repair stock-proof fences. These could be in the form of banks and ditches in which the bank was nearest the wood and the ditch was on the outside as shown in Figure 9. The bank was surmounted by a hedge or wall. Such banks and ditches, though found in the Sheffield area, were not as widespread as in areas further south and east, because of the availability of gritstone and sandstone from which substantial drystone walls could be built, which obviated the need for banks and ditches. There are numerous surviving references to wall repairs around local woods. In July 1719, for example, five wallers were paid £1-13-0 by the Duke of Norfolk's woodward for six days' work '...walling down Gapps and low places in Greno Wood fence' and in November 1838 wallers were busy 'gapping' in a large number of woods on the Duke's estate in Sheffield, Ecclesfield and Rotherham.

Hedgerows were also constantly being replanted around newly felled woods. In 1710 William Sheppard was paid one shilling and eightpence for '...hedging 2 days at ye far end of Shertcliffe Park new cutt' and William Walker and his partners were paid £1-19-8 for completing 136 roods of '...spring hedging betwixt Smithy Wood and Jonathan Wingfield's Closes'.

Even so, animals got into the woods and when detected they were impounded and the owner fined. In 1718 Enoch Moor was fined one shilling when nine of his sheep were '...pounded out of Greno Wood' and in 1720 two men were paid three shillings and sixpence by the Duke of Norfolk's woodward for their trouble in '...pounding 5 sheep belonging to Mr Watts that was trespassing in Little Hall Wood'.

The strong, high walls and thick hedges were usually proof against grazing animals in South Yorkshire, and no instance has been found in more than 600 years of records to match the exasperation of Thomas Watson-Wentworth's wood agent on visiting, in 1728, one of his employer's coppices in Co Wicklow in Ireland that had not been properly fenced. He observed that the wood had been '...Eaten as Bare as A Bowling Green'.

Holly hags

Occurring side by side with the coppice wood system in the Sheffield area throughout the Middle Ages and into the eighteenth century was the management of holly trees as winter fodder for farm stock, especially sheep, and for deer. The practice was not restricted to this area but seems to have been generally associated with upland farming areas in northern England. The holly woods, which were either small separate woods or compartments within woods or on wooded commons, were called holly hags. A hag is an old name for a coppice compartment. The holly hags must have been cut on a rotation like other underwood and then allowed to grow back.

The use of holly as winter fodder was recorded in the Sheffield area as early as 1442 when the Lord of Hallamshire's forester at Bradfield noted in his accounts a payment for holly sold for animal fodder in winter. John Harrison, in his survey of the Manor of Sheffield in 1637, recorded 27 separate 'Hollin Hagges' that were rented by farm tenants from the Earl of Arundel.

The custom of using holly as fodder was graphically described by two early travellers in the Sheffield area. In 1696 the diarist Abraham de la Pryme wrote that:

In south west Yorkshire, at and about Bradfield, and in Darbyshire, they feed all their sheep in winter with holly leaves and bark, which they eat more greedily than any grass. To every farm there is so many holly trees; and the more there is the farm is dearer; but care is taken to plant great numbers of them in all farms thereabouts.

Twenty-nine years later in 1725 a party headed by the Earl of Oxford travelled through Sheffield Park and out towards Hackenthorpe and Mosbrough. It was noted that they had travelled:

through the greatest number of wild stunted holly trees that I ever saw together. They extend themselves on the common...for a considerable way. This tract of ground they grow upon is called the Burley Hollyns...(They have) their branches lopped off every winter for the support of the sheep which browse upon them, and at the same time are sheltered by the stunted part that is left standing.

In the days before the widespread planting of fodder crops for serving to animals in winter, holly and other woody fodder from hedges and woods must have been important especially in the moorland fringes where stock could not be left to forage for themselves in deep and long lasting snows. In the winter of 1710 the Duke of Norfolk's woodward noted in his accounts that he had paid Henry Bromhead 'for him and horse going 2 days in ye great snow to see if any one croped Holling'. The impression given was that moorland edge farmers were in the habit, in hard winters, of cutting other people's holly. No doubt Bromhead had a blunderbuss over his saddle!

Holly hags also occurred in deer parks. In a lease of Tankersley Park in 1653 it was stipulated that the deer had to be fed by 'serving them with holley to be cutt therein in winter.' Early nineteenth century maps of the park show a field called the Far Hollings in the south-east corner of the park and a print of about 1730 shows a small walled wood in that location. Holly is still an important constituent of Bull Wood on the edge of Tankersley Park golf course and this may be the site of another Tankersley Park holly hag. Bull Wood is clearly shown on the 1730 print.

Wood pasture and its decline

Mention has already been made on several occasions of wood pastures. These were woods in which underwood and timber were harvested but in which animals were allowed to graze freely. As populations grew and settlements and therefore clearance of woodland increased, wood pasture declined and coppice management became predominant. However, wood pasture survived alongside coppices for many centuries. In the medieval period and beyond wood pastures were found in the Sheffield area on wooded commons, in deer parks and on chases.

Wooded commons were unfenced areas on which commoners (persons who held land in the open fields and had certain rights on the common land in the manor) had the right to graze their animals. Commoners usually had the right of the underwood but the timber usually belonged to the lord of the manor. In the manor of Sheffield in 1637 there were more than 21,000 acres of common, much of it wooded. Almost all of this disappeared at the time of the Parliamentary Enclosures between 1750-1830 and only fragments remain, one of the largest stretches being Loxley Common referred to about 1650 as 'one Great Wood called Loxley the herbage common and consisteth of great Oake timber'. About ten years earlier another wooded common, Walkley Bank, was said to have 'a great store of rough Oake trees & some bircke [birch] woods'. In the same year another wooded common, Stannington Wood, was said to consist of 'pt of rough Timber & pt of Springe wood'. A large part of the former Stannington Wood is now occupied by the grounds and playing fields of Myers Grove School, but part of the common is still wooded, though replanted, and forms Little Matlock Wood beside the River Loxley. The grazing in Stannington Wood and on Walkley Bank, like that on Loxley Common, was grazed by the commoners' animals.

Deer parks, large and small, sometimes well wooded and sometimes only moderately so, studded South Yorkshire in the medieval period. Unlike commons, deer parks were areas of private land, bounded by a wall or bank with a cleft-oak paling fence, in which the owner kept deer, hares and rabbits in order to provide his family with a reliable source of meat, and grew timber and underwood. There were more than 200 deer in Tankersley Park in 1653 and 1000 in Sheffield Park in 1637. In the eighteenth century many medieval deer parks were landscaped but often retained their herds of deer, often joined by sheep and cattle. Earl Fitzwilliam even kept buffaloes at one period! Parks contained coppice woods, (in this area including holly hags) and great timber trees. Tankersley Park was once renowned for its ancient oak trees, in one of which the 1st Earl of Strafford was supposed to have been arrested; the particular tree was actually identified on the first edition of the O S six-inch map published in 1855. Sheffield Park, its site now covered by housing developments at Park Hill, Norfolk Park, the Manor and Arbourthorne was also famous in its day for the size of its trees. John Evelyn in the second half of the

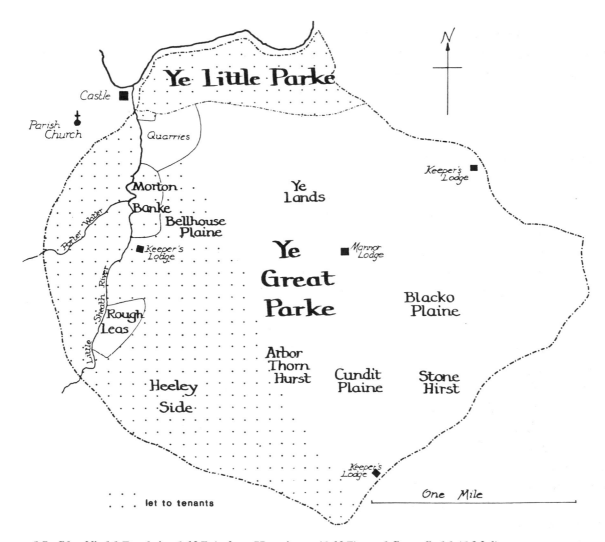

Figure 15. Sheffield Park in 1637 (after Harrison (1637) and Scurfield (1986). The medieval deer park contained 2462 acres and was eight miles in circumference. It had a typical shape, a rounded rectangle which was the most economic shape for fencing. By 1637 more than 971 acres had been let to tenants, including the whole of the Little Park, all that part of the Great Park to the west of the Sheaf, and all but two enclosures amounting to about 80 acres in the western third of the Great Park to the east of the Sheaf. The tenanted parts of the park were a mixture of arable, grazing and meadow, but also included a coppice wood (Morton Bank). They also included Heeley Side which was grazing land in which there were coal pits which Harrison in 1637 said 'yieldeth great profit unto the Lord'. The two enclosures within the tenanted parts of the park were the Quarries which were used to impound tenants' stray animals, and Rough Leas which were hay meadows 'for the deere and Mill horses'.

Those parts of the park still managed as a deer park, and containing 1000 fallow deer in 1637, were uncompartmented areas. The areas with woodland names (Arbor Thorn Hurst and Stone Hirst) were probably only wooded in places and probably scrubby. Other names (Ye Lands, Cundit Plaine, and Blacko Plaine) suggest treeless areas. Ye Lands is probably a corruption of laund. A laund was a grassy, treeless area in a deer park. The word plain had a similar meaning although it was usually employed to describe large glades in chases rather than parks. Ye Lands and the various plains probably contained thickets of hawthorn and holly (holly hags) and scattered trees, probably pollarded to protect the regrowth. The trees in Sheffield Park described by John Evelyn in the 1660s were of a girth and size that suggested that some at least were ancient pollards. For example, he described an oak tree in the park whose trunk was 13 feet in diameter and another 10 yards in circumference. On Conduit Plain (the Cundit Plaine of Harrison's survey) Evelyn said there was an oak tree whose boughs were so far spreading that he estimated (giving all his calculations) that 251 horses could stand in the shade of it!

23

seventeenth century in his book *Sylva*, described a massive oak tree growing below the Manor which provided 1400 'wairs', which were planks two yards long and one yard wide, and 20 cords (40 tons) of wood from the branches. The local woodward who reported it to Evelyn may have been exaggerating slightly! The same informant described to Evelyn another oak tree in the park, that was so big that when it was felled and lying on its side, two men on opposite sides of it on horseback could not see each other's hats. Sheffield Park as described by Harrison in his 1637 survey of the Manor of Sheffield is shown in Figure 15.

Wood pasture was also a feature of chases. Chases were areas of land, usually a mixture of heath, moor and woods of various kinds on manorial wastes, in which large landowners hunted wild animals, particularly deer, and in which there were strict regulations governing hunting, grazing, and wood and timber production and felling. They were the private equivalents of the Royal Forests. Unlike parks, chases had no fences and were often intermingled with settlements and farms. Rivelin Chase which belonged to the lords of Hallamshire, Wharncliffe Chase which belonged to the Wortley family, and Hatfield Chase which belonged to the de Warenne family of Conisbrough castle and later to the Crown are local examples. When Harrison surveyed Rivelin Chase, or Rivelin Firth as he called it, in 1637 he noted within its nearly 1900 acres 'ye Old Laund [grassy treeless area] reserved for ye Deare' and an area of particularly stately and ancient trees which occupied the sloping land between Stannington village and the River Rivelin. This was called Hawe Park by Harrison and today the site is partly occupied by Parkside Lane and Hallpark Farm. Harrison's description is worth repeating in full:

> *Item Hawe Parke lyeth open to Rivelin ffirth but it is at ye pleasure of ye Lord to Inclose it....This peice is full of excellent Timber of a very great lenght & very Streight & many of them of a great bigness before you come to a Knott in So much that it hath been said by Travellers that they have not seene such Timber in Cristendome .*

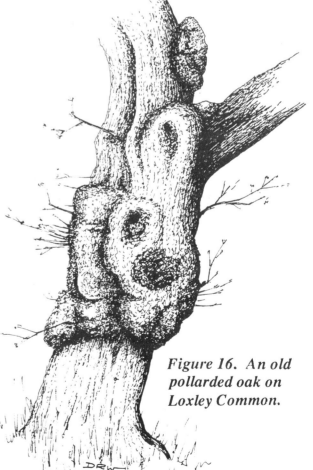

Grazing and tree growth do not go well together and on many commons and in parks and chases a special kind of woodland management was practised in order to produce underwood beyond the reach of grazing animals. This was called **pollarding**. In this form of management the trees were 'coppiced' at least six feet from the ground leaving a massive permanent lower trunk called a **bolling** above which a continuous crop of new growth sprouted out of reach of the grazing deer, sheep and cattle. There are still two old neglected pollards on Loxley Common.

Figure 16. An old pollarded oak on Loxley Common.

24

The decline of traditional woodland management

The decline of wood pasture management began, as has already been pointed out, in the Middle Ages with the expansion of coppicing, although it was still widespread on wooded commons and in deer parks in the seventeenth century as Harrison's 1637 survey shows. However it was already in decline.

As we have already seen, a substantial part of Sheffield Park was let to tenants by 1637 and eventually the whole park disappeared, first through its sub-division into separate farms, then through the spread of manufacturing and mining activity, and finally through the spread of the built-up area of Sheffield. Now virtually all that is left to remind us of its former presence are place names and the ruins of the Manor Lodge described by Harrison in 1637 as '...standing on a hill in ye midle of ye Parke being fairely built with stone & Timber with an Inward & an outward Court 2 Gardens & 3 Yards...'. Tankersley Park to the north of Sheffield also went into gradual decline. The hall in the middle of the park was abandoned and subsequently largely dismantled to provide building stone for a farmhouse for a farm that had been carved out of another part of the park. The park was then gradually encroached upon and disfigured by ironstone mining. There was still a herd of deer there in the 1850s even though most of the original park was by then a vast ironstone mining ground. The deer were eventually removed to Wentworth Woodhouse where there is still a herd of about 100 red deer. Other parks in the area were converted in the sixteenth or seventeenth century into coppice woods. In this category come Tinsley Park and Holmesfield Park.

Wood pasture on commons declined steeply in the second half of the eighteenth and the first third of the nineteenth century as commons were enclosed under the Parliamentary Enclosure acts. These 'new' enclosures on old commons are easily recognised in the western half of our area by their square and rectangular walled fields. Figure 17 shows Stannington Wood in 1637 and 1890.

Coppicing itself went into steady decline during the nineteenth century and had virtually disappeared in the Sheffield area by the beginning of the First World War. This decline was partly the result of nationwide changes but there were also important local factors that accelerated its decline in this area.

Nationally, the growth of the railway network and with this the widespread adoption of coal as a domestic fuel instead of wood affected those coppice woods where firewood markets were important. The growth of factory production and rapid and reliable distribution, again mostly by rail, meant that factory-made products often in metal where previously wood had been used, hit many local craftsmen badly and reduced the demand for coppice in some areas. Even where the factory products were still wooden, regional specialisation and large-scale organisation meant that the previously ubiquitous self-employed craftsmen found it difficult to compete, and gradually disappeared, leaving fewer markets for locally produced underwood. The demand for bark from tanners also declined as they took advantage of cheaper imported bark and chemical substitutes.

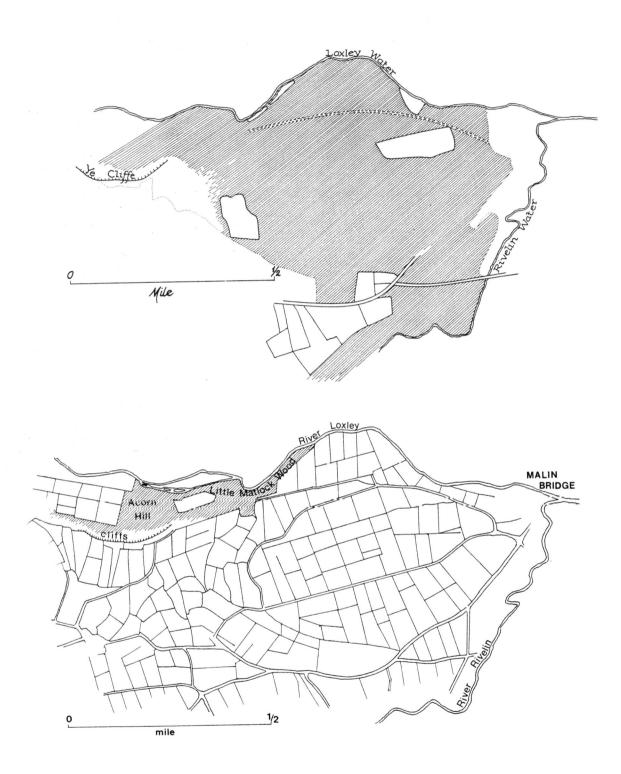

Figure 17. Stannington Wood in 1637 and the same site in 1890.

26

Locally the adoption in the eighteenth century by lead smelters, iron makers and some steel makers of coke instead of charcoal meant the loss of major markets. This, coupled with the presence of valuable coal and ironstone seams under many local woods, and the rapid physical growth of Sheffield led to the eventual destruction of centrally located woods and the further contraction of the coppicing tradition. Woods for which records of coppicing stretched back for at least 300 years, disappeared under housing and industrial development. The former Burngreave Wood survives only in the form of a few stunted oaks growing over a patch of bluebells in Burngreave Cemetery, and the former 53 acre Hall Carr Wood in Brightside has left nothing behind but its name. Other nails in the coffin of coppice management locally included the increasing amount of trespass from the growing urban population seeking recreation in the surrounding countryside, and the pall of pollution that hung over the city in the nineteenth century.

By the 1890s coppicing was nearing its end. Income from local coppices had declined sharply and management problems were increasing. As a result more and more woods were gradually converted into canopy woods or 'high forests'. In essence they were becoming plantations, and **forestry** was replacing **woodmanship**. This was achieved by singling the multi-stemmed coppice stools in order to allow the best stem to grow into a standard tree, by clearing away altogether the oldest stools and sickly trees, and in their place planting young trees to be grown for timber on a long cycle (see Figure 50B). Many of the newly planted trees were not native to the Sheffield area, trees such as beech, sweet chestnut, common lime and sycamore. Amongst the broadleaved trees, conifers were often planted as a 'nurse crop' for the slower growing broadleaves. For example, in October 1898 the Duke of Norfolk's forester began to systematically plant timber trees in large sections of local coppice woods. In Hesley Wood he planned to plant 100 acres with ash, elm, sycamore, birch, lime, sweet chestnut and beech eight feet apart and 'filled up' at four feet intervals with larch. That was 145,000 trees altogether! Another 100 acres were to be planted in the same way in Smithy Wood, 120 acres in Greno Wood, 60 acres in Beeley Wood, 40 acres in Bowden Housteads Wood, 25 acres in Hall Wood and 20 acres in Woolley Wood. Conifers were to be planted in all the woods mentioned above, but when he came to Shirecliffe Wood he noted that 'being situated nr Sheffield & therefore affected by smoke etc Larch & conifers would not grow well...'. On 16 November he placed his first order for young trees with a nursery in Cheshire. He ordered, for delivery at Wadsley Bridge Station, 20,000 larch, 10,000 sycamore, 5,000 beech, 2,000 birch and 2,000 sweet chestnut.

Forestry management, mostly in the form of coniferous plantings, has continued to be important right up the 1990s in some parts of the area and large woods such as Wharncliffe and Greno have been almost completely coniferised.

A large number of former coppice woods eventually came into the ownership of the City Council either as gifts or by purchase. Roe Wood was gifted to the City Council by the Duke of Norfolk in 1897 and Wincobank Wood was given by the same owner in 1904. Bowden Housteads purchased from the Duke in 1914 and Ecclesall Woods bought from Earl

27

Fitzwilliam in 1927 are just two examples of former coppice woods converted to canopy woods and then sold to the City Council.

The local authority woods are now mostly amenity woods, but since their purchase almost all of them have been managed only on a 'care and maintenance' basis and in consequence they have grown over-mature, dark, and their shrub layers have been greatly diminished or have almost disappeared completely (see Figure 50C). Some City-owned woods are managed by the Estates Department as commercial woodlands and these are managed as plantations. Gillfield Wood is such a wood. This ancient wood, first mentioned in 1561 when it was a coppice wood, has been completely transformed by the planting of sycamore, American red oak and larch.

Sheffield's woods are now at a cross-roads. If they continue to be un-managed or under-managed they will all continue to decline in quality and some will disappear altogether. If they are managed sympathetically they will last for at least another 1000 years.

PART 3: FORGOTTEN WOODLAND CRAFTS AND INDUSTRIES OF THE SHEFFIELD REGION

Felling the timber and coppice

Landowners with small woods on their land and timber growing in their hedgerows must have used a great deal of their crop on their own farms but larger owners, besides using large amounts of wood and timber on their own estates for their own and their tenants' use - including industrial tenants such as ironmasters, coalmasters and metal workers - also sold large quantities of coppice wood and timber on the open market.

When a wood or a compartment within a wood was going to be felled and sold on the open market, the sale was preceded by a valuation of the wood which involved marking the timber trees that were to be left standing and marking and valuing the timber trees that were to be felled. Among the former would be wavers that would be allowed to reach maturity before felling and mature trees that were being reserved for particular purposes and would be felled at another time. As the marking proceeded - this was called **setting out** - the timber trees to be felled would be given individual values and an overall value for the underwood was also computed. For example, in a valuation of Ladies Spring Wood on the Beauchief estate in 1823, 186 itemised trees valued at £258 were numbered to 'go down', together with 613 poles valued at £108. In addition it was calculated that there would be 312 quarters (just under four tons) of bark worth £218 and top and underwood (loppings from the poles and timber trees) worth £48. The valuer got a fee of over £20 calculated on the basis of fourpence for every £1 of the valuation together with an allowance of eight shillings and sixpence for oil and paint used in marking the timber trees.

Handbills and contracts from the Beauchief and Duke of Norfolk's estates in the eighteenth and early nineteenth centuries show that at that period much of the underwood and timber destined for the open market were sold by tender. Surviving documents allow us to follow one such sale, in a compartment at Hall Wood belonging to the Duke of Norfolk, from beginning to end. The first stage was to set out the wood, i.e. to value it and decide which trees were to be felled and which were to remain. In the case of the Hall Wood compartment it was decided to leave standing 1,290 mature trees and 2,015 wavers and these were marked with white and red paint respectively and numbered using a special tool called a scribe iron. The timber trees to be felled, 230 in number, were again numbered with scribe irons but not painted. The sketch which forms the cover and frontispiece of this book shows marked trees in a Sheffield wood. Also for sale were 1,567 underwood poles, of which 1,460 were oak, 100 birch and alder and 7 ash.

The next stage was to advertise the sale and this was done through handbills like the one in Figure 18. At the sale, which was normally held at a local inn, the woodward would write the estate valuation on a ticket and put it folded on the table in front of him. Within a specified time all those wishing to tender for the timber and underwood and any other woodland products included in the sale, such as bark, had to put their bids on separate tickets (one ticket per bidder) and place them on the table. This was done three times, on each occasion the woodward announcing the name of the highest bidder. The highest bidder on the third occasion became the purchaser provided the bid equalled or exceeded the valuation. If it did not, the highest bidder

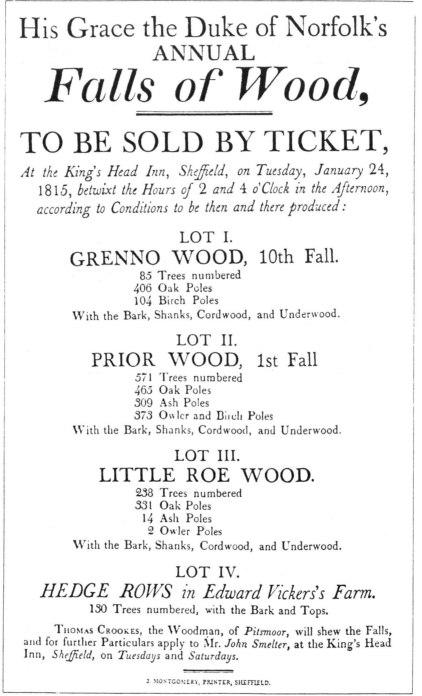

His Grace the Duke of Norfolk's
ANNUAL
Falls of Wood,

TO BE SOLD BY TICKET,

At the King's Head Inn, Sheffield, on Tuesday, January 24, 1815, betwixt the Hours of 2 and 4 o'Clock in the Afternoon, according to Conditions to be then and there produced:

LOT I.
GRENNO WOOD, 10th Fall.
85 Trees numbered
406 Oak Poles
104 Birch Poles
With the Bark, Shanks, Cordwood, and Underwood.

LOT II.
PRIOR WOOD, 1st Fall
571 Trees numbered
465 Oak Poles
309 Ash Poles
373 Owler and Birch Poles
With the Bark, Shanks, Cordwood, and Underwood.

LOT III.
LITTLE ROE WOOD.
238 Trees numbered
331 Oak Poles
14 Ash Poles
2 Owler Poles
With the Bark, Shanks, Cordwood, and Underwood.

LOT IV.
HEDGE ROWS in Edward Vickers's Farm.
130 Trees numbered, with the Bark and Tops.

Thomas Crookes, the Woodman, of *Pitsmoor*, will shew the Falls, and for further Particulars apply to Mr. *John Smelter*, at the King's Head Inn, *Sheffield*, on *Tuesdays* and *Saturdays*.

J. MONTGOMERY, PRINTER, SHEFFIELD.

Source : ACM S 300

Figure 18. Handbill announcing falls in the Duke of Norfolk's woods to be sold by ticket in 1815.

was given the first option of buying at the estate valuation. Figure 19 shows the successful bid for the Hall Wood sale in 1823 and Figure 20 shows an unsuccessful ticket. The successful bidder was described as a steel burner from Grenoside. In some sales the timber, underwood and bark were bid for separately.

In the case of the Duke of Norfolk's woods, once contracts were signed the purchaser was given about 12 months to fell the trees and underwood, using only approved woodmen, and another six months in which to cart them away. If in the felling or carting operations trees marked to stand

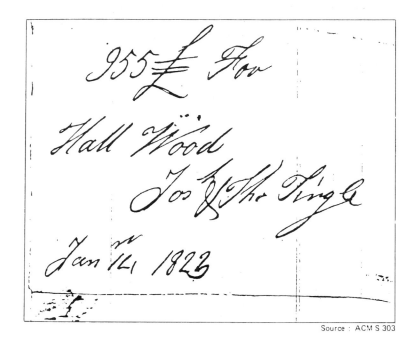

Source : ACM S 303

Figure 19. The successful ticket at the 1823 fall in Hall Wood.

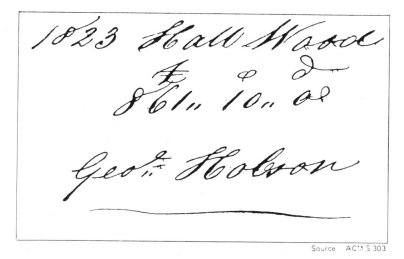

Source ACM S 303

Figure 20. An unsuccessful bid for the same fall.

31

were injured or felled in error, other trees had to be left in their place or appropriate compensation paid. Purchasers were also instructed to leave the stools of the underwood in 'a growing state after cutting', and if charcoal was being made from the underwood the charcoal makers had to use only the turf (for covering the charcoal stack) specifically provided by the Duke's woodward. Sawpits were also provided.

Once felled the underwood was treated in different ways depending on how it was going to be used. Tall underwood poles to be used as hop poles and in making ladders had their branches removed and then left as they were. Stout poles to be used as punch wood (pit props) were also left in various lengths. On the other hand, underwood that was to used in charcoal making was cut into four feet lengths and stacked in piles eight feet long and four feet high. Such piles each contained about two tons of wood and were called **cords**. Figure 21 shows a partly completed cord in a Kent wood in 1987. Firewood was also sold by the cord.

Figure 21. A Kent chestnut coppice with a partly completed cord.

The smallest branches and twigs from the trees and coppice, generally called brushwood and spray, was called **ramelia** in medieval Latin documents but by the seventeenth century in the Sheffield area the English equivalent **rammel** was being used and this is still the word used by many people in Sheffield to mean rubbish. This material was not wasted but bound together into **faggots**. Faggots were used as the fuel in fires requiring high temperatures in a short period. They were commonly used to heat bakers' ovens, which were then scraped clean and the dough put in. In 1719 there is a record of **kids**, one of the smallest sizes of faggots, being used to burn bad meat in Sheffield market. Faggots were made in large quantities, and in 1720, 1,000 kids were made from the tops of trees felled in Scraith Wood for the use of the Duke of Norfolk's tenants.

Some large timber trees were selected for special purposes and their felling was a major event. Figure 22 shows a very large oak tree being felled in Greno Wood in the early years of this century for Greaves' saw mill and furniture factory at Charlton Clough near Chapeltown. Out of sight of the observer at the back of the tree the two woodmen would already have cut at the base of the tree, with saw and axe, a large notch called a **bird's mouth** or **sink** to direct the tree away from them when it fell. Then kneeling on opposite sides of the tree as comfortably as they could, each woodman would pull, then rest on the other man's pull, pull, rest and so on until the tree fell away behind them. The **wedges** are being knocked in to lift the tree off the saw as the felling proceeds.

Figure 22. Felling an oak tree in Greno Wood, from a photograph taken about 80 years ago.

Once felled and cut to length or sawn as necessary, the trees and underwood and their by-products were dispersed to be put to an amazing number of uses, some of which are described in more detail below.

Timber as a building material in the Sheffield Region

Many visitors to the Sheffield region think that the traditional building material is stone. The walls, roofs, door jambs and window sills of ancient parish churches, country seats of the aristocracy and the gentry, old farmhouses and cottages, ruined castles and the remains of abbeys and priories appear, with a few exceptions, to be constructed almost entirely of local gritstone, sandstone or limestone. What is forgotten is that the limestone keep at Conisbrough Castle and the many medieval stone churches in the region were probably replacements for wooden

33

structures and that the stone walls of many surviving medieval minor buildings replaced or still encase a timber frame. Moreover, in old stone or brick buildings, the sandstone roofslabs or pantiles rest on a substantial framework of locally grown timber.

In fact it was not until the seventeenth century in the Sheffield region that stone supplanted timber as the main building material, and there still remain in Sheffield Metropolitan District about 75 pre-1700 buildings of timber frame construction, and many more built of stone but with medieval timber roof trusses.

It is in these buildings that trees from the region's medieval woods can be seen. I say trees because in the Middle Ages the carpenter did not buy his timber in the form of ready sawn and shaped planks and beams, he selected trees in woods and hedges that would roughly square up to the dimensions of the components required with the minimum of shaping. For great beams a large tree of 60-75 years of age with a diameter of 15-18 inches would be chosen, and for rafters much younger trees about eight inches in diameter would be felled.

The timber used was almost always oak and it was sawn or shaped with an axe or adze while it was still 'green', for ease of working, as shown in the celebrated scenes from the Bayeux Tapestry reproduced in Figure 23, and carpentry techniques were developed to capitalise on the natural shapes and properties of the trees.

Figure 23. Eleventh century woodmen, carpenters and shipwrights in the Bayeux tapestry.

Three surviving medieval buildings have been chosen to show the use made of trees of different dimensions, carpentry techniques, and the two basic types of timber-framed building found in the Sheffield area: Kirkstead Abbey Grange at Thorpe Hesley, Bishops' House at Meersbrook and the barn called Oaks Fold in Concord Park. Kirkstead Abbey Grange is a stone building, now subdivided into three houses, whose roof contains some of the most interesting late medieval carpentry in south Yorkshire. Bishops' House is a museum and the timbers and carpentry, both inside and out, can be studied in some detail. The barn in Concord Park is used by the City Recreation Department to store equipment and it can be inspected by permission of the park staff.

34

Kirkstead Abbey Grange, so named when it was restored in 1900 by the Earl of Effingham, was formerly known as Parkgate Farm. It is popularly thought to be a Norman building constructed in the second half of the twelfth century by the monks of Kirkstead Abbey in Lincolnshire who had been given permission in 1161 by the lord of the manor to mine and smelt ironstone in Kimberworth township and to build a dwelling there. A detailed survey by the South Yorkshire County Archaeological Service in 1984 has shown that the building has a very complicated history and is late medieval rather than Norman, but incorporates stone and timber features from an earlier building, possibly the original one built by the Kirkstead monks in the late twelfth century. Figure 24 shows the building in 1893, seven years before it was restored. The left hand (southern) half of the building was the house and the right hand (northern) half, the barns. The round-headed doorways that led to the belief that it was Norman can be clearly seen.

Figure 24. Kirkstead Abbey Grange in 1893.

Figure 25 shows the roof structure of the southern end of the building. It is a **king post** roof, a type that is almost wholly confined to the north of England. In this kind of roof a series of king posts (A in Figure 25) rise from **tie beams** (B) which rest on either timber framed or, as in this case, stone walls. Rising from each end of the tie beams are **principal rafters** (C) which are fitted into the top of the king posts with mortise and tenon joints. Running from king post to king post and supported by **braces** (D) are **ridge pieces** (E). Halfway down the principal rafters are **purlins** (F). This superstructure supports a large number of **common rafters** (not shown in the diagram), running from the ridge piece to the top of the wall, which in turn support the roof covering, in this case sandstone slates.

In its original state the roof consisted of 212 timber components, all oak, including the shaped trunks of 183 individual trees! Most of it has survived, only rafters and purlins having been

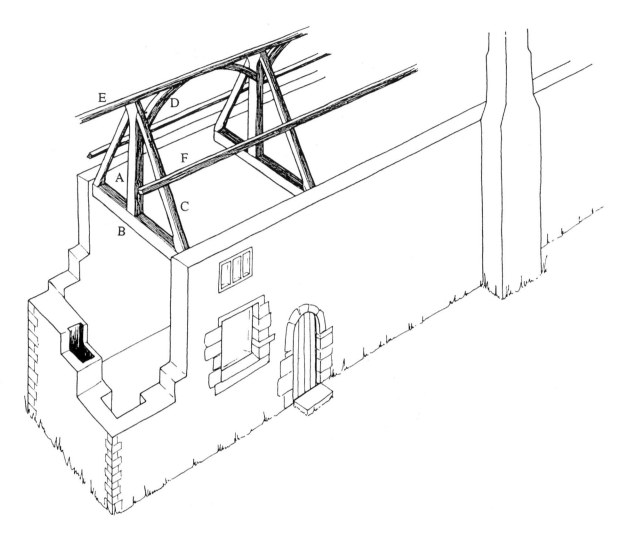

Figure 25. The roof structure at the southern end of Kirkstead Abbey Grange.

replaced in parts of the roof in the 1900 restoration and the more recent (1985) conversion. More than 84 per cent of the trees used were less than nine inches (23 cm) in diameter and only 11 per cent (the tie beams and the trees from which the principal rafters were sawn) measure more than 12 inches (30 cm) in diameter.

Detailed studies in East Anglia have shown that ordinary medieval buildings contain few timbers more than 20 feet (6 m) long and those that are longer are often crooked, knotty and tapering, showing that the carpenter was using every inch of the upper part of the trunk in order to gain extra length. At Kirkstead Abbey Grange the tie beams are a little over 18 feet long from wall to wall so that together with the ends that rest on the walls (which are about 32 inches thick) they must be nearly 20 feet long. However, the tie beams are exceeded in length by one other member. The ridge piece extending northwards from the southern end of the roof is 22 feet long. At its northen end it is 7 x 7 inches in section and this must represent the **butt end** (bottom) of the trunk, because it tapers southwards, gradually losing its square section and becoming **waney** (rounded at the corners through reaching the outside of the log) as shown in Figure 26.

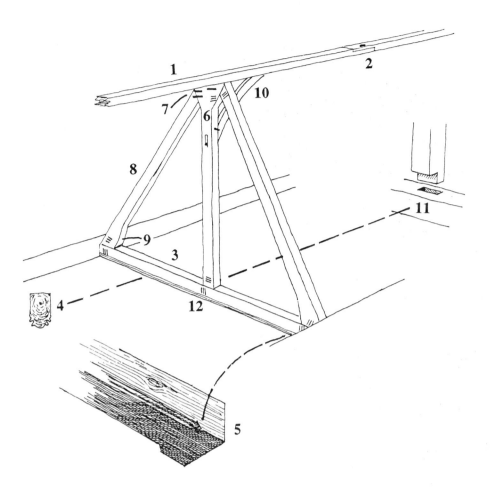

Figure 26. Details of the roof structure at Kirkstead Abbey Grange.

1. *Ridge piece tapering towards south and becoming waney.*
2. *Scarf joint.*
3. *Cambered tie beam.*
4. *Section through tie beam showing roll moulding.*
5. *Beam stop.*
6. *King post with jowled top.*
7. *Treenails securing principal rafters to king post.*
8. *Pair of principal rafters probably sawn from one trunk.*
9. *Shoulder at foot of principal rafter.*
10. Curved brace
11. Barefaced tenon.
12. Carpenter's marks in Roman numerals (III).

It was obviously important to fit together the individual ridge pieces so that they formed one continuous strong component running the whole length of the roof. The joint used in these circumstances was the **scarf joint**, and the one joining the ridge piece just described to the next one is also shown in Figure 26. The joint was originally held together by a vertical wooden key (now missing).

A number of other interesting and unusual aspects of the use of timber and the skills of the medieval carpenter can be illustrated by a closer inspection of the roof truss that is labelled in Figure 25 and whose details are shown more clearly in Figure 26. The first thing to note is the tie beam. It is a knotty timber some 14 x 9 inches at its most massive central point and it has a slight but obvious symmetrical curve or camber on its upper side. Its underside (called the **soffit**) is not curved but is decorated by a roll moulding running almost its entire length. At its eastern end the roll moulding ends in what are called **beam stops**. The king post which is seven feet high is square for most of its length but at the top it widens to form what are called **jowls** to make it easier to accommodate the heads of the principal rafters which are held in place by long wooden pegs called **treenails**. Treenails, are used throughout the roof to secure joints, except where modern timbers have replaced the original ones. The principal rafters are interesting in that in section they are 10 x 5 inches suggesting that they are a matching pair sawn from the same squared trunk which was originally 10 x 10 inches. The trunk in fact must have been more massive than 10 x 10 inches at its butt end because just before reaching the tie beam the principal rafters develop broad shoulders which are quite unusual features. Originally, two matching curved **braces** from the king post to the ridge piece helped to strengthen the truss but only one has survived. The braces would have been specially shaped from naturally curving timbers. All the joints in the truss are mortise and tenon joints but the tenons are what are called **barefaced tenons**, that is the tenons have only one shoulder instead of the the usual two.

A final noteworthy feature of the truss is the marking done by the carpenter. The truss would have been put together on the ground, perhaps on the site, but more probably in the carpenter's yard or in a wood. It was then marked with Roman numerals, knocked down, and then reassembled on top of the walls, using the marks to ensure that every part was in its correct place.

Bishops' House, an L-shaped yeoman's house built c 1500-1550, has, like Kirkstead Abbey Grange, a king post roof, but whereas the latter is a stone building with an ancient timber roof, Bishops' House was originally completely framed in timber, although the timber framing on the ground floor has been largely replaced by stone, and a northern extension to the west wing was built in stone in the mid-seventeenth century.

The original timber-framed house had two wings (Figure 27 A), the east wing containing the hall and the kitchen open to the roof, and the west wing with a parlour and buttery on the ground floor and two chambers above on the first floor.

Both wings have a post and truss structure in which the king post roof is supported on a frame of vertical and horizontal oak timbers tied together, like the roof at Kirkstead Abbey Grange, with mortise and tenon joints and treenails (Figure 27 B). The timber framing originally continued almost to the ground, but at ground floor level, except for the principal (corner) posts, this has been replaced by stone. As a protection against damp the principal posts all originally stood on large stones called **stylobates**, some of which can still be seen, and the lowest horizontal timbers (**sill beams**) rested on low stone walls.

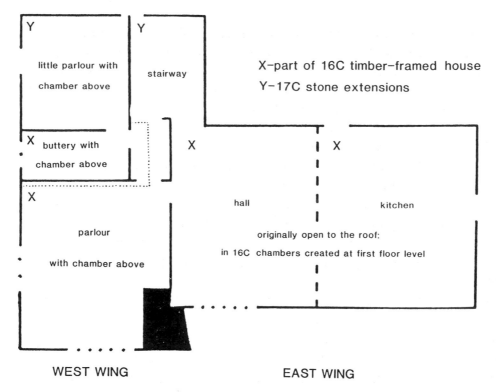

Figure 27A. Ground plan of Bishops' House.

Figure 27B. Post and truss structure of the kind at Bishops' House.

1 stylobate or padstone
2 principal post
3 tie beam
4 sill beam
5 girding beam
6 wall plate
7 brace
8 stud

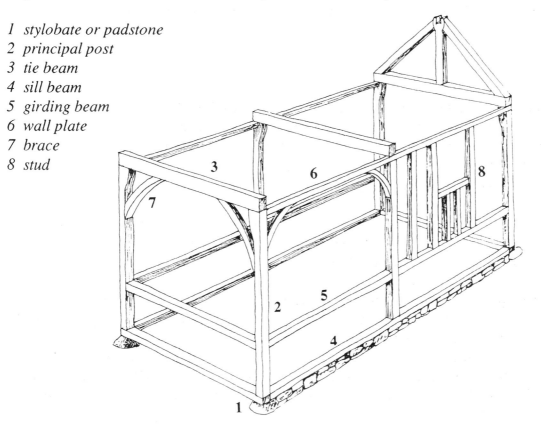

As Blore's drawing of 1823 shows (Figure 28), a variety of patterns of timberwork was employed. Herringbone patterns were employed on both wings, but that on the east wing points downwards and that on the west wing upwards. What is very noticeable everywhere on the building is that the timbers (**studs**) are closely spaced, with the spaces between them not much wider than the studs themselves. This **close studding** is a typical feature of timber framed buildings in the north of England. The spaces between the studs in timber framed buildings were filled with a variety of materials including wattle and daub, and stone slates covered with plaster. At Bishops' House split oak **laths** were fixed horizontally into grooves cut into the sides of the studs then covered with plaster.

Inside the house, features worth looking for are the carpenter's marks on the first floor wall of the west wing (X on Figure 27A), the adze marks on the shaped timber beside the stair head (Y on Figure 27A), the thick oak planks used to make the floors when upper rooms were put in the east wing in the seventeenth century, and the elaborately carved oak panelling of seventeenth century date in the hall on the ground floor of the east wing.

Figure 28. Bishops' House in 1823 as drawn by Edward Blore. The east wing is on the right and the west wing on the left.

Oaks Fold Barn in Concord Park is constructed quite differently from Kirkstead Abbey Grange and Bishops' House. It is a **cruck** building.

40

Cruck buildings are common in the upland areas of Britain and in parts of the Midlands but are virtually unknown in the east and south-east. Whether this indicates that they were never built there or were superceded at an early date by more sophisticated building methods is still an open question. In South Yorkshire there are only three records of cruck buildings in the zone to the east of Rotherham, but to the west of the town there are records of nearly 150 cruck buildings either still standing or known to have been demolished since 1900.

In a cruck building, as shown in Figure 29, the weight is carried on pairs of timbers called **cruck blades** which rise from or near the ground and meet at the apex of the roof. The blades are

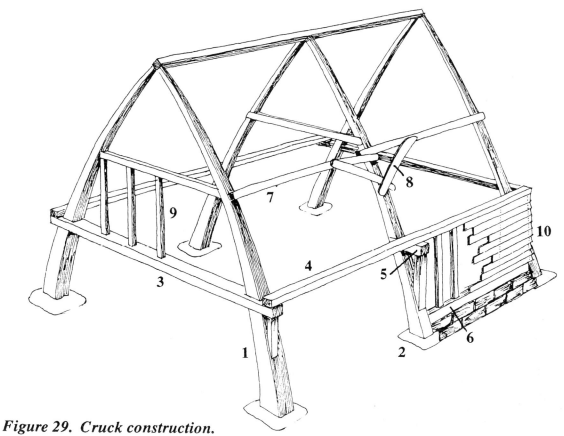

Figure 29. Cruck construction.

1 *cruck blade*
2 *stylobate or padstone*
3 *tie beam*
4 *wall plate*
5 *spur*
6 *sill beam*
7 *purlin*
8 *wind brace*
9 *stud*
10 *oak boarding*

usually curved, having been selected from naturally bent trees. Often a bent tree was split or sawn lengthways to make two matching blades. The structure is strengthened by tie beams connecting each pair of blades. If it was not convenient to have tie beams across the interior of the building, the **wall plates** were carried on **spurs** projecting from the back of a cruck blade and supported on a short vertical post. The roof of the building was stabilised by struts called **windbraces**. When such buildings had timber walls, the ends of the tie beams carried longitudinal wall plates. In the timber walls vertical studs rose from sill beams to the wall plates. The gaps between the studs were filled with a variety of materials, as already noted, or, alternatively, the entire wall could be covered by horizontal oak boarding.

The Oaks Fold barn was described by John Harrison in his 1637 survey of the manor of Sheffield. He recorded 'ye tenement called Woolley Grange alias Oakes Farme with a dwellinghouse & a Barne of 5 bayes'. A **bay** is a space between each pair (in this case six) of cruck blades. Woolley Grange derives its name from the fact that it was originally a farm belonging to Ecclesfield Priory.

The barn has long been encased in stone, and when that was done the wall plates became redundant and most were removed. Most of the windbraces have also disappeared. However the cruck blades are on full view and at the far (west) end of the barn, as shown in Figure 30, some of the lath and plaster wall filling can still be seen.

Figure 30. The interior of Oaks Fold cruck barn looking west, from a photograph taken in October 1988.

Charcoal and whitecoal making

The preparation of charcoal for use as the fuel for iron smelting is the oldest recorded woodland industry in the Sheffield region. In a deed dated 1161, already referred to above, Richard de Busli, the lord of the manor of Kimberworth, granted the right to Kirkstead Abbey in Lincolnshire to mine, smelt and forge iron in Kimberworth. In the deed, which is in Latin, de Busli specifically gave the monks permission to collect dead wood in Kimberworth to fuel their smelting hearths - *...mortuum nemus de Kymberworth quantum sufficit illis quatuor ignibus...* ('... enough dead wood from Kimberworth for all four furnaces...'). The wood would not have been used in the form that it was collected but would have been converted into charcoal ('coaled') first.

Two other medieval documents referring to charcoal making in the local area have survived. In 1462 two local men, John Cotes and John Parker, were given permission to 'cole' the underwood in a number of places in the Gleadless Valley, including the present-day Rollestone Wood, and in 1496 the Abbot of Beauchief Abbey gave permission to Roger Eyre to fell the coppice in Hutcliffe Wood and to convert it into charcoal for use in iron smelting. A copy of the deed, which is in English, can be seen in Sheffield Record Office and it specifically mentions that a place had been allocated for the making of charcoal:

> *'...beryn wyttenes that the forsaid Abbot and Convent have...lett to the said Rogr a bloom harth with a cool rowe and the Smethy Dam with sufficient ground to ley the stone apon...'.*

A bloom hearth was a primitive furnace, the stone was the iron ore and the 'cool rowe' was the place where the charcoal fuel was to be made.

A list of the Earl of Shrewsbury's woods in the Sheffield area, that was written sometime between 1598-1616, explicitly states that they were woods belonging to the Earl's forges, suggesting that their most important product was charcoal. 43 woods are listed in the manors of Sheffield, Ecclesfield, Handsworth, Tankersley, Kimberworth, Rotherham, Whiston and Treeton and a number of them are stated to be 'coalable' or 'redie to be coled'.

Surviving records show that in the seventeenth and eighteenth centuries woodland owners were entering into long term contracts with local ironmasters. For example, in 1657 Lionel Copley, a Rotherham ironmaster, entered into a contract with the second Earl of Strafford of Wentworth Woodhouse which covered 13 woods over a ten year period. Among the woods included in the contract were three Sheffield woods: Tinsley Park which then covered over 400 acres, West Wood and Thorncliffe Wood. Under the contract Copley was to cut 1000 cords of wood (a pile of wood four feet by four feet by eight feet) each year for charcoal making. The deed in question, which deals in great detail with the cutting of the underwood and the collecting of the turves and dust for sealing the charcoal stacks, can be seen in Sheffield Record Office. At the end of this contract in 1666 Copley entered into a similar one with the Duke of Norfolk and the original deed is in the Archives and Local Studies Section of Rotherham Library.

The first Marquis of Rockingham, a descendant of the the Earl of Strafford, was in the fortunate position of having both ironstone and extensive woodlands on his estate and he linked the mining of the former with the charcoaling of the latter. This policy was helped by the fact that Chapeltown furnace, which was on land leased from the Duke of Norfolk, stood just down the hill from the Marquis' Tankersley estate which contained the easily mined Tankersley ironstone. In 1745 the Marquis wrote in his rental book:

> ...and whereas it is the Iron Men that keep up the Price of the Wood, Especiall care must be taken that the Iron Stone be never let for a longer time than the Woods are agreed for, because as none of the Duke of Norfolk's Estate affords Iron Stone nor none other nearer than Rockley the Duke's Works at Chappel Town cannot be wrought but with the Iron Stone of Tankersley by which Advantage if care be taken thereof they must be obliged to give a good Price for the Woods for the Sake of having the said Iron Stone...

A year later the Marquis was able to write, with obvious satisfaction:

> ...a new term of 11 years to Michaelmas 1758 was agreed upon for the Iron Stone & for all the Cord Wood for the same term at nine Shillings Per Cord...

Although the market for charcoal as the fuel for iron smelting gradually disappeared during the eighteenth century with the introduction and spread of the use of coke, some markets remained and others expanded in the Sheffield region. Most importantly, charcoal was used in making blister steel in so called cementation furnaces where successive layers of bar iron interbedded with layers of charcoal were heated up to high temperatures for up to eight days. Over 250 such furnaces with their characteristic conical chimneys were built in the Sheffield area of which only one remains in its complete state at the former Daniel Doncaster works in Hoyle Street. Another industry based on charcoal present in the region was gunpowder manufacture which used charcoal from alder, willow and alder buckthorn trees. In the nineteenth century there were works at Worsbrough Dale and at Wharncliffe. Charcoal was also used as blacking by moulders in iron foundries and the last known charcoal burner in the Sheffield area, William Ogden of Charlton Brook near Chapeltown, who died in 1911, was employed by Newton Chambers to produce charcoal for their foundries at Thorncliffe for this purpose.

During the coaling season, which usually lasted from April to November, charcoal burners, or **wood colliers** as they were earlier called, lived a solitary life, often with their families about them, deep in the woodlands.

Their work consisted of burning stacked lengths of coppice poles in the absence of enough air for complete combustion. The moisture was driven off during the early part of the process followed by volatile elements such as tar and creosote. The process left behind a residue of black carbon in solid form together with a little ash.

Figure 31. Charcoal using cementation furnaces in Sheffield in the late nineteenth century.

The spot where the burning took place, which was called a **pitstead**, **pit** or **hearth**, was about 15 feet in diameter and from it the turf was removed. There are different traditions of building the stack. One way, which was described in John Evelyn's book *Sylva*, published in 1664, and which may be a southern tradition, began with the laying on the ground of three short billets of wood in the form of a triangle. Other billets were added on top of the first three as shown in Figure 32 to form a central flue. A northern method, recently demonstrated in the Lake District, was to drive in a long central stake which was removed when the stack was ready. This is illustrated in Figure 33.

Figure 32. A method of beginning to build a charcoal stack.

45

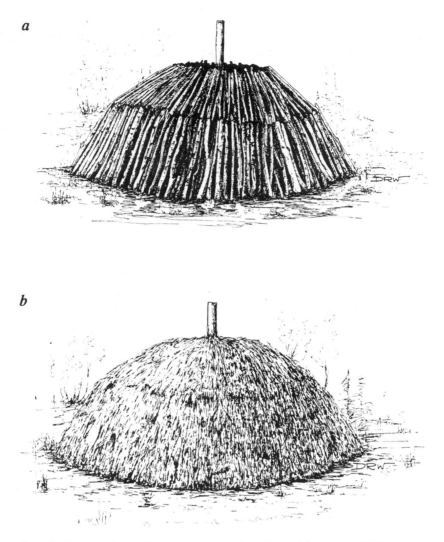

a

b

Figure 33. Completed charcoal stacks with central poles which would be removed in order to drop burning charcoal into the centre of the stack. Fig 33 (a) shows a stack immediately after stacking has been completed and Fig 33 (b) shows a stack covered by turves.

Whichever method of flue construction was used, the remainder of the stack was constructed by stacking cordwood lengths (billets four feet long), on end and facing inwards, around the central triangle or stake. This was continued until a stack was built up about fifteen feet in diameter and about five feet high in the shape of an inverted pudding basin (Figure 33 (a)). The wood was then covered by straw, grass, bracken and turves which were in their turn covered by dust and ashes. In this way virtually all air was excluded (Figure 33 (b).

If a central pole had been inserted this was now removed and red hot charcoal and a few dry sticks were dropped down the central flue. Once assured that the stack was alight, the wood collier sealed the flue and the fire would spread throughout the stack.

It was important that the stack burned steadily and that the fire did not burn through. For this

46

reason the charcoal burner had to be in constant attendance, protecting his charge from sudden wind changes with hurdle fencing and sacking and closing any gaps in the stack with bracken, turf and soil.

Burns lasted from two to ten days depending on size, weather conditions and the greenness of the wood. At first, as shown in Figure 34, the stack emitted clouds of white smoke, which gradually turned to a blue haze and then died away altogether. When the burn was over, the stack was uncovered with a rake, allowed to cool and then packed in sacks or panniers.

Figure 34. The early stages of a charcoal burn with thick white smoke. Note the hurdle protecting the stack from blustery winds.

Local deeds of the sixteenth, seventeenth and eighteenth centuries are full of the rules and conditions governing the gathering of coverings for the charcoal stacks. For example, a deed about the felling of trees in Anston Stones Wood near Rotherham in 1553 states that the lessees were to be allowed 'turfe & hyllyng for the colyng of the said wood'. A deed relating to Ecclesall Woods in 1649 allowed the tenants to 'have & take fodder & earth, fearns and other needful things' for covering the charcoal stacks and the agreement between Lionel Copley and the Earl of Strafford in 1657 already referred to, stipulated that if the tenant took 'dust, sleck or clodds' from other tenants' land, then those tenants could make good their land by taking more soil and turf from the commons.

It has already been emphasised that charcoal burners had to live more or less on top of their work and this could lead to fatal accidents. The only obvious remaining physical evidence of charcoal making in local woods is the wood collier's grave in Ecclesall Woods shown in Figure 35. Was it a sudden storm in the middle of the night that blew sparks from the stack onto his crude shelter? Or did he come back from the Rising Sun on Abbey Lane the worse for wear and fall asleep with his clay pipe still alight? (Sampson Brookshaw, the last named person on the gravestone was the landlord of the Rising Sun). Interestingly, William Ogden the last known charcoal burner in the Sheffield region also died while attending a burn in Lincolnshire. It is said that while sleeping near his stacks the wind changed direction and he was overcome by fumes.

Figure 35. Charcoal burner's gravestone in Ecclesall Woods.

He was probably sleeping in a crude hut next to the stacks. Fortunately photographs have survived, one of Shirecliffe Park Wood taken in about 1895, one in woods at Rockley taken in 1916, and one whose location is unknown taken about 1900 which all show charcoal makers' huts. All the huts were conical in shape probably built on a framework of poles like a wigwam and with a lintel lashed over the space left for the doorway. Over this framework of poles flat turves were laid in the manner of tiles. No door is shown in the Shirecliffe Park photograph but the one of Rockley shows a stake driven into the ground a few feet from the entrance; the door consisted planks of wood battened together which could be pulled in front of the doorway at night and merely pushed outwards to rest on the stake when the charcoal maker emerged in the morning (Figure 36).

Figure 36. A charcoal burner's hut of the type photographed locally at the end of the nineteenth century.

Alongside charcoal making in local woods between the last quarter of the sixteenth century and the middle of the eighteenth century was another woodland industry also making a fuel for smelting ore. This time the ore was lead and the fuel was called **whitecoal**. A number of local landowners including the Earls of Shrewsbury, the Strelleys of Beauchief and Ecclesall and the Brights of Ecclesall and Whirlow, are known to have been very active in the lead trade during that period. They obtained ore from the Derbyshire Peak District, smelted it in water-powered smelters called ore-hearths near their Coal Measure oakwoods and then transported the lead to the Humber for sale in the London market.

No one, as far as I know, has ever seen any whitecoal. It has not been made for over 200 years and is not likely to have survived or be recognised if it has. It was small lengths of wood, say six inches by two inches, dried in a kiln until all the moisture was driven out. William Linnard, in his book *Welsh Woods and Forests*, says that charcoal and whitecoal were mixed together in lead smelting because 'charcoal made too violent a fire, and wood alone was too gentle'. The former presence of whitecoal making in a local wood is betrayed by the presence of characteristic depressions, about four to five metres in diameter with a noticeable spout at one end. The spouts always slope downhill. These are the remains of the **whitecoal kilns**. It is not clear what they looked like when complete or exactly how they worked. They occur mainly on streamsides, usually on steep slopes and never on flat or wet ground. They occur in woods in the Coal Measure country of North-east Derbyshire and adjacent parts of South Yorkshire. They can be found in the Gleadless valley woods, in the woods on the former Beauchief Abbey estate, in Gillfield Wood at Totley, and in Ecclesall Woods where there are more than 80.

Oak bark leather tanning

During the 150 year period between 1680 and 1830, the production of leather and leather goods was, by value, the most important industry in England after textiles, and one of the largest employers outside agriculture. Woodlands played a significant part in this important industry by supplying tree bark which, before the introduction of chemical substitutes, was the major agent used in the preparation or 'tanning' of the animal hides before their conversion into such everyday articles as boots, shoes, clogs, harnesses, saddles, breeches, aprons, gloves, mittens, bags, cases and bottles, and for use in industry in bellows and belting. Book binders were also important consumers of fine leather.

Figure 37. The country tanner. *Note the large unglazed opening behind him to allow the free flow of air in what was a very smelly process.*

50

The tannic acid from ground bark seeps slowly through the pores of a hide, draws out the water and coats each fibre with a preservative. Although bark from other trees was used in the tanning process, the tannin content in the bark of oak trees made oak bark the most efficient and therefore the most important tanning agent. The woods in the Sheffield area were predominantly oak woods and they became associated with the leather tanning industry at an early date. Many of the surviving management records for local coppice woods include references to the peeling and selling of bark.

At a fall, most of the bark was peeled in large pieces from both the timber trees and the underwood poles. This was done by scoring a tree round its trunk at about two feet intervals and then making a longitudinal slit along the trunk. The bark could then be levered off in large plates with a bark peeler called a **spud**. It was often the practice to remove as much of the bark as possible while the tree was standing, then felling it to strip the rest (Figure 38). Some bark remained on the trees, especially around branches, and these were worked by other peelers, and their product was sometimes called 'pickt bark'. Bark was also knocked off old, decaying trees. The peeled bark was stacked to dry and then, as tannin is soluble in water, it was protected from rain until it was sold to tanners.

Figure 38. Peeling bark with a 'spud'.

For Treeton Wood in Rotherham in 1710 the whole process from the letting of the peeling contract to the selling of the bark to tanners is preserved in the account book of the Duke of Norfolk's woodward in Sheffield Record Office:

> ...Pd for Ale when we let the Pillings 00-01-00
>
> Pd Thomas Lee & partners for pilling 1420 fathoms of bark 18-14-05
>
> And for Stacking the same 2-07-04
>
> Spent at Treeton when I met the Wath Tanners 00-01-00
>
> Pd Mr Turner for 104 Thack Sheaves for thatching Bark stacks 00-4-04
>
> Pd Jno Clayton for covering 5 Bark stacks with Sods and 11 Stacks Covered with Straw 00-14-00
>
> Jno Oldam bought 100 quarts of Bark from Treeton Wood 16-13-08
>
> Lyonel Keyworth bt 62q & 2 f of Bark from Treeton Wood 10-09-09...

'Jno Oldam' was John Aldham, a member of a well-known tanning family from Upperthorpe in Sheffield.

At the tanyard the animal hides were first washed and cleaned up, usually in a water pit (Figure 39). This was followed by immersion in pits in slaked lime to open the pores on the hides to

OAK-BARK TANNING

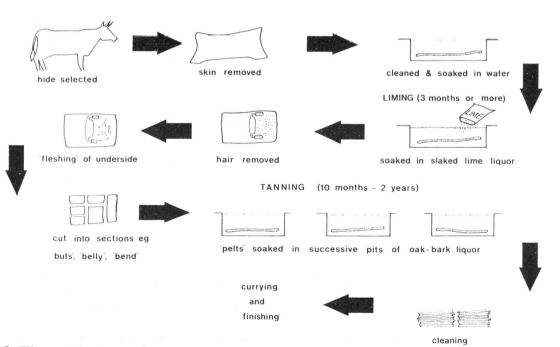

Figure 39. The oak bark tanning process.

facilitate the removal of hair. Hides were also 'baited' at this stage which meant soaking them in a solution containing dog excreta, hen manure or pigeon droppings. The hair and any remaining lumps of flesh were then removed using special dehairing and fleshing knives while the hide was lying over what was called a fleshing beam. After rinsing, the hides were cut into sections known as heads, necks, shoulders, bends and butts. They were then ready for the tanpits.

In the meantime the bark had been ground in a bark mill worked either by horse- or water-power. The ground bark was added to cold water to make the tanning liquor. The hides were then passed through a succession of tanpits, with increasingly strong tannin solutions. The hides were suspended in the pits from sticks or a wooden framework and care was taken that they did not touch one another so that they did not display touch marks or be uneven in colour. After several weeks of this treatment the 'half-tanned' hides were placed in so-called layering pits containing the strongest liquors of all. They were then dried, rolled and oiled before being sold to curriers for the final dressing and colouring.

Tanning was a skilled, complicated and protracted operation. Capital investment was high since a well maintained set of premises was a prerequisite of a successful tanning operation, and large numbers of hides and large amounts of oak bark were involved in the lengthy process. The probate inventory of William Aldham of Upperthorpe compiled in 1696 showed that he had £400 worth of leather in stock and 'in ye pitts'. The inventory of another member of the Aldham family compiled two years later, showed he had 327 hides in stock worth over £150. The advertisement shown in Figure 40, from the *Sheffield Iris* in 1797, describes a typical local tanyard at the end of the eighteenth century.

The harvesting of oak bark and its use in leather tanning continued to be important until the closing decades of the nineteenth century. In 1882 over 62 tons of oak bark from Hall Wood,

---

HANDSWORTH WOODHOUSE
Sale of Farming Utensils.
TO BE LET A complete and
Large Tanyard well-supplied with
excellent water, good bark house,
bark mill, drying kiln and house.
Five miles from Sheffield.
Advantageous both for the purchasing
of bark and the extensive trade now
carried on.
Apply Mr. Newbould upon the premises.

Figure 40. An advertisement for the lease of a local tanyard from the Sheffield Iris, 27 October, 1797.

Parkin Wood and Woolley Wood in Sheffield and from Canklow Wood and Treeton Wood in Rotherham were sold to Henry Clegg of Barnsley who by that time was the only major purchaser of oak bark from local woods. In the 1881 census Henry Clegg was described as a 'Tanner, Currier, Leather Merchant, Mill Strap and Boot upper Manufacturer'. He employed 23 men, six boys, one woman and two girls and owned two tanneries at Cawthorne and Denby Dale.

The small crafts

The felling of timber and coppice, bark peeling, leather tanning, charcoal making and whitecoal production were conspicuous woodland industries over a long period of time. Less well-known but once widespread locally are a number of specialised crafts that have disappeared completely from the area because either there is no longer a general demand for them, or because the objects once produced in wood are now made from metal or plastic, or because the former domestic crafts have become large-scale industries and production is now concentrated in factories. Such crafts include turnery, coopering, wheelmaking, clog making, basket making, thatch spar making, rake making and besom making. Another dozen crafts could be added to the list including such unlikely ones as boatbuilding and birch wine making. Boatbuilding was still carried on by two small firms at Worsbrough Dale well into the nineteenth century and they were both regular customers for timber from Sheffield's woods. For about a decade from 1717 Sarah Lockwood of Stannington leased the right of obtaining sap from birch trees in Stannington Wood, for ten shillings a year. The sap, which would have been collected in spring when the sap was rising by cutting a slit in the trunk under a branch, was mixed with honey, cloves, lemon peel and ale to make a mead-like wine.

Turners made not only wooden dishes and plates, but also a wide range of kitchen and dairy implements. With the advent of cheap china, plastics and stainless steel, and the almost complete disappearance of domestic butter and cheese making, the turner is now more likely to be producing decorative objects or toys, often in imported woods. Until 40 years ago turners also made dolly pegs and wringer rollers, but these objects are no longer required in an age of automatic washing machines. The turner worked on a simple lathe called a pole lathe and worked in woods such as rowan (it was supposed to have magical properties), elm, ash, birch, beech and sycamore. By the nineteenth century sycamore was the wood most commonly used because it does not taint foodstuffs, it can be repeatedly immersed in water without warping or cracking, it has a pale colour without any marked figuring, and it can be worked and turned while green. Medieval court rolls, records of marriages in local churches from the late sixteenth century to the early nineteenth century, and early census returns all mention turners, dishturners and dishmakers.

Like turners, coopers also made vessels for food and drink. There were three branches of coopering: dry coopers manufactured casks to hold non-liquid goods such as flour, tobacco, fruit or even gunpowder, white coopers made articles for domestic and dairy use, and wet coopers, the most specialised branch, produced casks for carrying liquids. The dry cooper used a whole range of timbers, the white cooper worked in oak, sycamore and ash, and the wet cooper only in oak. Much oak timber from Sheffield's woods in the past was turned into staves for coopering work. No homestead before the nineteenth century would have been without a small number of specialised vessels made by a local cooper: **pails** and **piggins** for carrying water and milk, **churns** for making butter, tubs called **keelers** for cooling liquids, tubs called **kimnels** for general use, lidded **kits** for holding milk, butter and other foods, and **hogsheads** for storing ale. The inventory of William Blythe of Bishops' House at Meersbrook compiled in 1665 included two barrels, nine half hogsheads 'with some beare in', one flour kit, three flesh kits 'with some meate in them', two churns, two kimnels and a cheese tub.

Figure 41. Wet coopers.

Wooden soled footwear was common in the past, not just for wearing in factories and coal mines but for everyday wear and for when working on the farm. There were two distinct crafts: clogmaking and clog sole cutting (clogging). Clogmakers were also often boot and shoemakers using the wooden soles provided by the cloggers who bought trees and converted them into rough-cut soles. The cloggers used alder, willow, birch, sycamore and beech trees. Alder was the preferred timber because it is water resistant and easy to work. Trunks were cut into short logs that were about the same lengths as the four standard sizes: men's, women's, children's and middles. These short logs were then riven (split) into sole blocks using a mallet called a **beetle** and a metal wedge, and finally shaped with a special tool called a **stock knife** which was attached by a hook at one end to a ring on a low bench as shown in Figure 42. The Dronfield family at Grenoside were well-known local cloggers in the nineteenth century. William Dronfield Junior (died 1916) was a regular buyer of alder, sycamore and birch trees from the Duke of Norfolk's woods in Ecclesfield parish. He also made the beetles for the Duke of Norfolk's woodmen and brush heads.

Another woodland craft that is associated with Grenoside is basketmaking. The Sharpe family were basketmakers there in the nineteeenth century and there are references in the Duke of

Figure 42. A clogger shaping clog soles with a stock knife.

Norfolk's wood accounts of the Sharpes being given permission (wood leave) to cut hazel and willow rods in local woods. They also bought oak coppice poles probably for swill making as described below. Their small pond where they soaked willow rods prior to weaving them into baskets and other kinds of basketwork is still in existence in an area called "Sharpes' wood 'oil".

A locally made type of basket used by, among others, charcoal burners,was the **spelk** or **swill**. This was made by weaving thin strips of oak (spelks) around a hoop of ash or hazel. The spelks were obtained by boiling oak coppice poles and riving them while still hot. Two of these baskets can be seen in the foreground in the drawing of the charcoal burners that forms the cover and frontispiece of this book.

Besom making was also a widespread local craft until the beginning of this century. Besoms were indispensible for sweeping flagged cottage floors, factory floors, and dirt roads and paths. The besom handles were made from young ash, birch and hazel poles and the brooms were made from bundles of birch or hazel twigs, or from heather, tied together originally with strips of willow, riven oak or even bramble. Later wire was used. The manufacture of a besom is a simple and short task - something like 10 minutes - when performed by a skilled 'broom squire', as besom makers were called. A production rate of ten dozen a day was not unusual.

Figure 43. Chopping the butt ends of birch twig besom brooms.

The way in which local woodland crafts were being progressively 'industrialised' and taken out of the small woodland communities in which they had been created and perfected is shown by the advertisement below (Figure 44) for Garsides' saw mill and factory at Worksop in 1853. The factory was a regular customer for timber and coppice poles at wood sales in the Sheffield area.

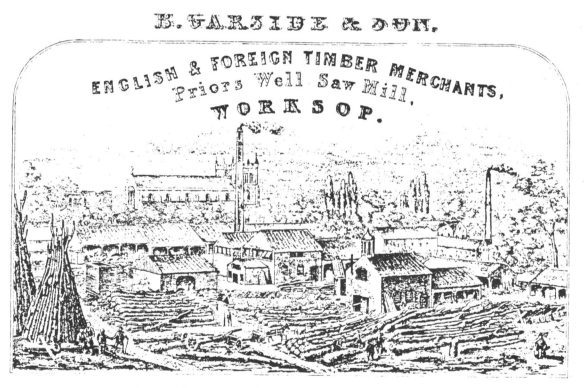

Figure 44. An advertisement for B. Garside & Son's sawmill and wooden handle factory at Worksop, From R. White's Visitor's Handbook to Worksop & its Neighbourhood, 1853.

PART 4: SHEFFIELD'S WOODLANDS TODAY: WHAT THEY CAN TELL US ABOUT THEIR PAST

In spite of name changes, partial clearance, the complete disappearance of traditional management practices, the planting of exotic broadleaved trees and conifers, and neglect, the careful study of large-scale maps and **SLOW** walks around and through surviving local woods at all seasons of the year can reveal a great deal about their history. The clues to look for are their names, their positions, their shapes, their boundaries, their internal man-made features, and the types and distribution of trees, shrubs, herbs, grasses and sedges that grow in them.

Woodland names

The two clues most obviously looked for in the names of woods are indications of age and former function.

Past cultures all had distinctive names for woods: the Celtic *coed* usually corrupted to chet or cet; the Old English *fyrth* (firth or frith), *graf* (grove), *hurst* (copse or wooded hill), *sceaga* (small wood, now written 'shaw'), *wudu* (wood) and *spring* (coppice wood); the Old Norse *lundr* (grove), *skogr* (wood, written now as 'scough'), *with* (wood), *storth* (coppice wood) and *carr* (wooded marsh); and the Norman-French *copeiz* (coppice).

Wood names that incorporate the names of villages, townships or parishes are also taken to be names of considerable antiquity, for example Ecclesall Woods and Hesley Wood.

There are, of course, difficulties with all these names; some old names have been lost and replaced by modern ones; other names were used through successive periods, and the terms wood and copse, for example, have been used to name new plantings right into the present century. It is therefore necessary to study old maps and surveys and to consult place-name dictionaries in order to be sure that what appears to be an old name is not a modern invention. Two local examples illustrate the name substitution problem. The name 'Buck Wood' for the wood behind Gleadless Road on the Gleadless valley estate is relatively new. In John Harrison's survey of the manor of Sheffield of 1637 it was called Berrystorth, an old Norse name suggesting an ancient origin, but by the last quarter of the nineteenth century the old name had been replaced by the modern name which, unlike its predecessor, tells us little of its past. It has already been pointed out that old parish or village names in wood names are usually reckoned to indicate an ancient origin. On this basis it might be thought that Treeton Wood in Rotherham bears an old name. But this is not so. The present name appears to be a late eighteenth or early nineteenth century successor to the much older 'Oaken Cliff', the name by which it was known throughout the seventeenth century. The older name tells us something about both its composition and its site.

Despite these problems any local wood carrying a name including one of the Old English, Old Norse or Norman-French names listed above, or a settlement name, is worth investigating. It is probably an ancient wood (in existence since at least 1600) and is most probably the descendant of an old coppice wood.

The most common names of Old English origin are *wood* and *spring*. *Wood* is a bit of a problem. It was used over a long period of time, it was used to replace older names and it has continued to be used right up to the present time for new plantations. *Spring* is more useful in that it indicates coppice management at some point in a wood's history, but it does not necessarily mean a wood is ancient. The term 'spring wood' was in common use until coppice management died out locally at the end of the nineteenth century. For example, Newbiggin Plantation at Tankersley, which was planted in the early nineteenth century to hide coal and ironstone mining spoil heaps, was listed under Earl Fitzwilliam's spring woods a few decades later. Among local woods bearing the name *spring* and known to be ancient are Low Spring at High Green, Wilson Spring between Birley Edge and Oughtibridge, Snaithing Spring in Ecclesall, Ladies Spring Wood at Totley, and Newfield Spring Wood in the Moss Valley. The value of consulting old maps or written surveys is shown by seventeenth and eighteenth century records relating to Ecclesall Woods. The overall name tells us little beyond the location of the woods, but the old surveys show that they were subdivided into numerous compartments for coppicing purposes, and some of the compartments were called springs, for example, Dobbe Croft Spring and Bright Spring. The first name is commemorated today in Dobcroft Road and Dobcroft Avenue. The 'Bright' in the second name is a family name. The Bright family owned Ecclesall Woods from the middle of the seventeenth century until 1752 when Mary Bright married the 2nd Marquis of Rockingham and the woods became part of the Wentworth Woodhouse estate until they were bought by the City Council in 1927.

The Old English element *fyrth* is found in local documents in connection with wooded chases and commons. Rivelin Chase is referred to in Harrison's survey of 1637 as 'Revelin ffirth' and there is a document surviving from 1558 which refers to the 'Fyrthe of Westnall' in Bradfield which was a wooded common. There is a Frith Wood at Coal Aston and Greno Wood was once known as Grenofirth.

Old Norse names, like Old English names, are widespread locally. The element *lundr* corrupted to lound and lund has survived in the district names of Lound Side in Chapeltown and Lundwood in Barnsley. The wood that gave the Lundwood area its name was referred to in a document written in 1541 as the wood called *le high lunde*. The term *carr* is another Old Norse woodland name that has survived as a general place name, as in Deepcar. When applied to woods it described lowlying woods bordering streams and rivers in which alders and willows predominated. There is a Carr Wood between Heeley and Gleadless. It occupies the narrow valley of a tributary of the Meers Brook and was referred to as 'Carr Wodd' in 1583. The word alder itself is also found in local place names. Its local form is *owler* as in Owlerton and Owler Lane. Both *carr* and *owler* are preserved in the name Owler Carr Wood in the Moss valley.

Storth, or storrs as it is usually now written, is another Old Norse element that is widespread. Besides being a wood name, it is used in stream names, names of hamlets and farms, and it is still a not uncommon surname in South Yorkshire. Its widespread distribution not only reflects the heavily wooded nature of parts of the area in the past but also the strength of Old Norse words in the evolving South Yorkshire dialect. Reference has already been made to Berrystorth (now Buck Wood) in the Gleadless valley. Harrison in 1637 also described a wood called Kent Storth, and there is still a Brownstorth Wood at Troway in the Moss valley. The element is also used in the name of the hamlet of Storrs between Stannington and Dungworth (where there is a Storrs Wood), in Storth House near Holmesfield, and in Storrs Dike which is the boundary stream of West Wood, an ancient wood at Tankersley. It is also the old name of many fields in South Yorkshire, indicating where woodland was cleared in the early medieval period. In Harrison's 1637 survey, for example, there are more than 20 references to fields called storth or storrs. The field on either side of the path leading to Gillfield Wood at Totley is called Storth Leys (coppice wood clearing).

The element *copeiz*, of Norman-French origin, is also preserved in or near local woods, for example in Scholes Coppice near Rotherham and in Coppice Wood, Coppice House and Coppice Farm in the Rivelin valley. The element also occurred in the form 'coppy wood' as the name of a compartment in Ecclesall Woods in the eighteenth century.

Woodland names also reflect ownership, tenancies and functions. Prior Royd at Grenoside and Priest Wood and Prior Wood, which are old names for parts of Beeley Wood, strongly suggest ownership at some period by a religious house - in these cases by Ecclesfield Priory. Those woods that carry a personal name indicate owners (e.g. Lord's Wood (lord of the manor's wood) and Bright Spring), woodwards (e.g. Wilson Spring named after Thomas Wilson the keeper of woods at Grenoside in the seventeenth century) or tenants as in Wheata Wood in which the Whete family had tenant rights in the late fifteenth century, and Parkin Wood at Chapeltown where the Parkin family were tenants in the seventeenth century.

The positions of woods

Old woodland is often in remote places in a parish, in farthest corners and right on parish boundaries. It is also often on windswept hill tops, broad ridges and steep slopes and in narrow valleys, especially if they contain springs. This complements the early pattern of settlement and cultivation: as farms, hamlets and villages were established and woodland cleared for grazing and cultivation, the surviving woods acquired a scarcity value. Naturally the more remote and difficult sites were more likely to survive.

A close look at the positions of ancient woods in Ecclesfield parish illustrates the point. Figure 45 shows the woods as they existed in 1810 before they were affected by mining and clearance for road development and settlement expansion. The large number of woods (25 in all) is unusual, as is the total woodland acreage of over 1500 acres. What is more remarkable is that almost all the woods have survived to the present day, if somewhat reduced in size, changed in

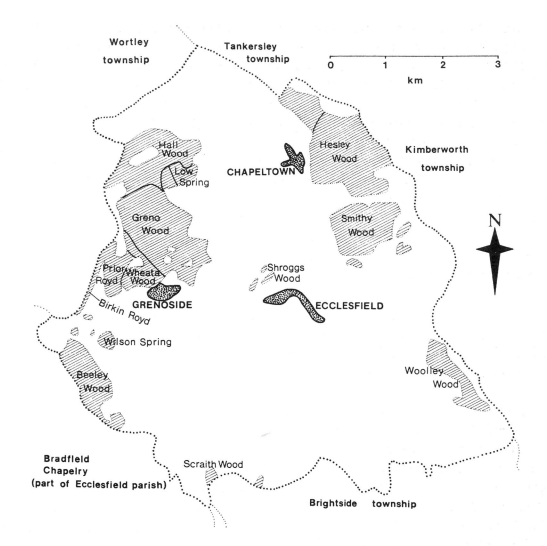

Figure 45. Ancient woods in Ecclesfield parish in 1810.

shape, and usually either neglected or planted with conifers or non-native broadleaves.

Looking at the parish as a whole, only the three small woods to the north of Ecclesfield village did not occupy parish edge locations. Hall Wood has an interesting name when its location is considered. The name may be derived from *hale* which in Old English means 'at the corner'. The location of the wood would justify this name. Besides their parish edge locations, many of Ecclesfield's woods occupy sites that would not have been amongst the most desirable for cultivation and settlement. Parts of Greno Wood rise to over 1000 feet and other woods are on very steep slopes. Birkin Royd seems almost vertical in places. *Scraith*, in Scraith Wood, means scree, a steep, boulder-strewn slope, and the early name of Scraith Wood was *Scryhcrest*, possibly a corruption of *Scrith-hurst*, reflecting its high, steep site above the middle Don valley. Other woods, although not occupying precipitous slopes, are on fairly steep valley sides as at Parkin Wood, Woolley Wood, Beeley Wood and parts of Prior Royd and Hesley Park.

61

Parish edge locations on steep slopes are repeated elsewhere in the Sheffield area. West Wood and Thorncliffe Wood at Tankersley occupy steep valley sides above Blackburn Brook, and Hutcliffe Wood, Park Bank Wood, Old Park Wood, High Wood and Ladies Spring Wood all lie on steep slopes in the Sheaf valley. The element *cliff* in the names of local woods as in Thorncliffe, Hutcliffe and Shirecliffe (a large lost wood) is a reminder of steep slope locations. 'Hang Bank' in Hang Bank Wood at Gleadless simply means steep slope.

There are, of course, exceptions to these generalisations, and Ecclesall Woods, for example, although on a parish edge, lie on generally moderately shelving ground on unbroken terrain.

Woodland shapes

Ancient woods are those parts of the original woodland cover, much modified by man, that remained when land had been cleared for cultivation, for pasture and for settlements. They are, therefore, 'left overs' that have been attacked by axe and saw over a very long period of time from different directions by different cultures. Periods of rapid onslaught must have alternated with periods of inactivity as population growth gave way to stagnation, therefore lowering the demand for farmland, fuel, building materials and so on. It is not surprising, therefore, that old woods commonly have irregular shapes, unlike modern forestry plantations which tend to have straight sides and regular shapes.

Ancient woodland edges tend to be sinuous or else zig-zagged with well marked peninsulas and bays like a rocky coast, as if giant bites had been taken from them. This unevenness is the result of the unplanned, piecemeal clearing process, which in the medieval period was known as **assarting** and resulted in the creation of small irregular fields. Where such fields were created from clearing woodland the process may be reflected in their names. *Intake* (land reclaimed from the waste), *ridding* and *royd* (land cleared of trees) and *stubbing* (land cleared of trees but with the stumps remaining) all testify to the woodland clearance process. Small fields carrying names meaning wood such as storth or spring or the name of a particular wood, together with close (enclosure), also point to the removal of part of a wood, or even a whole wood, in the past.

These features of curving or zig-zagging woodland boundaries abutting on irregularly shaped fields with names indicating woodland clearance are widespread in the Sheffield area and can be illustrated by the adjacent woods of Birkin Royd, Prior Royd and Wheata Wood at Grenoside (Figure 46). It is as if a giant pastry cutter has been at work with the three woods representing the left-over pastry. The surrounding field names include eight intakes, two stubbings and one royd. To the south of the woods are Stanley Hill (Stanley = stony woodland clearing), Stubbing House and Birley (byre or cowshed clearing). Andrew Carr Farm in the same area was described in a lease of 1484 as 'three acres of assert land'.

Boundary and internal earthworks

The need to protect coppice woods from beast and man has already been discussed at some

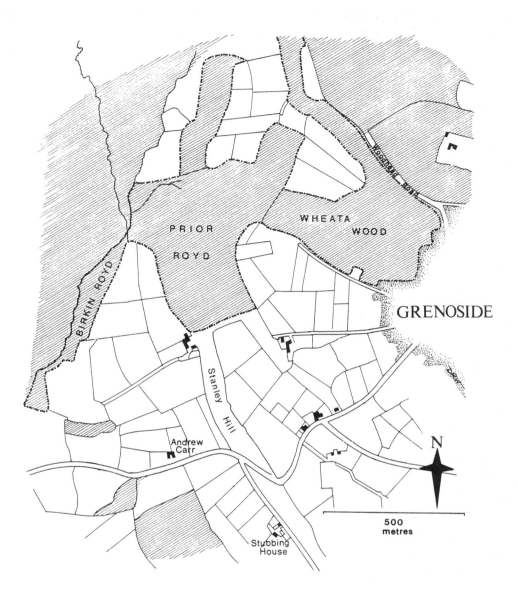

Figure 46. Ancient woodland shapes at Grenoside.

length in Part 2. People, of course, could break down hedges and climb walls and so it was in order to prevent uncontrolled grazing by domestic animals that led owners to erect barriers around woods.

In the counties of eastern England such as Lincolnshire, Norfolk and Suffolk, where outcrops of rock are absent over large areas, the woodland boundaries were normally in the form of banks and ditches with the ditches on the outside. The higher and broader the bank and the deeper the

63

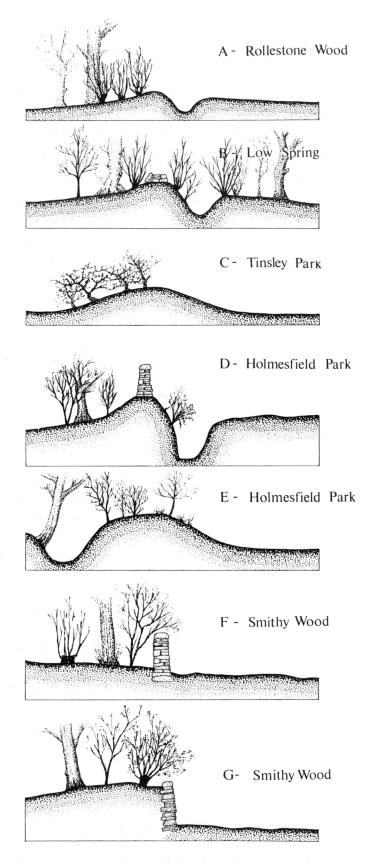

Figure 47. Examples of ancient woodland boundaries in the Sheffield area.

ditch, the older it is likely to be. In East Anglia some ditches are as deep as six metres and banks are as much as eight metres across. Thick hedges or wooden palisades often surmounted these banks and where trees grew on them they were often pollarded so that grazing animals in neighbouring fields could not feed on the new shoots. In areas where good building stone outcropped at the surface, stone walls took the place of banks and ditches. In the Sheffield area both ditched banks and, much more commonly, stone walls are found around old woods.

Among places where banks are to be found in the Sheffield area are Park Bank Wood at Beauchief, Low Spring at High Green, Rollestone Wood at Gleadless, Tinsley Park and Holmesfield Park. The banks at Park Bank Wood and at Rollestone Wood (Figure 47A), which both have external ditches, surround only short sections of the wood. The low and narrow bank at Low Spring (Figure 47B) bounds the northern edge of the wood and separates it from Hall Wood. It was originally topped with a wall, of which only the footings remain. In contrast, the bank at Tinsley Park (Figure 47C) is broad but there is no external bank. At Holmesfield Park there is a large wood-bank with a deep external ditch on the western margins of the wood, (Figure 47D) but, more interestingly, along part of the eastern edge there is a massive bank with the ditch on the inside (Figure 47D). This bank appears to date from the period when the wood was a deer park, and the arrangement with the ditch on the inside was to keep the deer in rather than to prevent domestic animals from entering the park from adjacent fields and lanes. At Smithy Wood freestanding stone walls and walls built into natural banks have survived round the woodland (Figure 47F and G).

Earthworks in the form of depressions, ditches and banks also occur inside woods. They may tell us something of the economic activities connected with a particular wood or they may suggest that a wood is secondary, the original wood having been cleared at an early date for settlement or cultivation or some other economic activity and then allowed to revert to woodland.

Large coppice woods were sub-divided for management purposes and as the coppice poles in the various compartments were at different stages of development, animals may have been allowed in some parts of the wood and not others. In such circumstances internal walls, hedges or ditched banks with hedges or walls were necessary. Ecclesall Woods were subdivided into as many as 20 smaller coppices at various times and today some of the internal boundaries can be detected by the winding low banks within the wood (not to be confused with the equally numerous artificial drainage channels) which probably once supported hedges.

Ecclesall Woods also contain more than 80 mysterious depressions, which also occur in Gillfield Wood at Totley, the Beauchief woods and the Gleadless valley woods. These depressions are four to five metres in diameter and have spouts at one end. They are mostly, but not always, on sloping ground near streams. Documentary evidence suggests that they were kilns in which **whitecoal** was prepared. This was kiln dried wood used as the fuel in water-powered lead smelting hearths between about 1575 and the mid-eighteenth century. A whitecoal kiln in Gillfield Wood is shown in Figure 48. Sites levelled for charcoal stacks are more difficult to

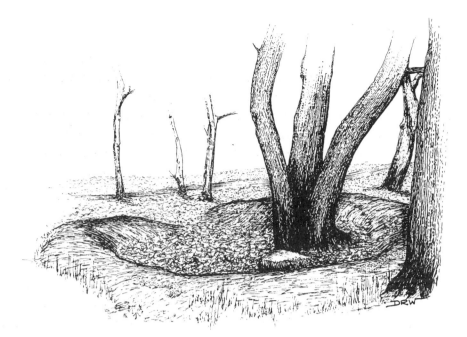

Figure 48. A whitecoal kiln in Gillfield Wood.

identify and depend upon finding accumulations of charcoal and evidence of habitation (see Part 3). Careful searching reveals substantial numbers of these in Ecclesall Woods.

Evidence of mining for both coal and ironstone, and of quarrying for stone may also be found in local woods. Evidence of past mining activity is usually in the form of large shale mounds with central depressions. These mark the locations of former bell pits. In bell pit mining a shallow shaft was sunk and the mineral extracted immmediately around it and then a new shaft was sunk a short distance away. The mineral was wound to the surface by windlass or horse gin. Such pits were being sunk in the local area from very early times right up to the middle of the nineteenth century. When the M1 motorway was being built through part of Smithy Wood near Chapeltown in the 1960s many bell pit shafts were found. These are believed to be of medieval origin associated with the iron mining and smelting activities of the monks of Kirkstead Abbey who were active at Thorpe Common just to the east of Smithy Wood as early as the 1160s.

Many older earthworks also survive in some local woods and suggest that although the woods may be ancient they are unlikely to be direct descendants of the primaeval wildwood. In Scholes Coppice, for example, there is an Iron Age camp. The earthen ramparts suggest a defensive refuge of some kind and recent excavations have discovered evidence of post holes for what was probably a wooden palisade, so it is unlikely that the defenders would want to be surprised by attackers creeping up on them through a wood. The wood, therefore, seems to have regenerated after the camp was abandoned. A similar situation occurs in Wheata Wood where settlement sites dating from the first to the fourth centuries AD have been discovered.

Woodland trees and shrubs

Beech, hornbeam, the two native limes, sweet chestnut, sycamore, red oak and most conifers are

66

not native to our area. The two native limes appear to have become extinct locally at an early date, as did Scots pine. Of the conifers, only yew is locally native. Beech and hornbeam are both native trees, but wild beech and wild hornbeam are trees of southern England, not the north Midlands. Large-leaved and small-leaved lime reach their natural northern limit to the east of Sheffield. They both occur in the Rotherham area and small-leaved lime is found in a wood in the Moss valley but I know of no Sheffield wood in which they naturally occur. Sweet chestnut was introduced from the Mediterranean probably by the Romans. Conifers such as larch and Scots pine were introduced (or re-introduced in the case of the latter) as timber, ornamental, or shelter belt trees. Sycamore was introduced in late medieval times. The earliest local record I have found of a sycamore tree is in Handsworth in 1712. Sycamore has now become naturalised and is spreading invasively into and through woods and tends to shade out young native trees.

What then are the typical trees and shrubs of Sheffield's old woods? The most widely distributed tree is the oak, more specifically the sessile oak (*Quercus petraea*). This oak, which is the common oak of northern and western Britain is uncommon in the south and east of the country. The sessile oak has stalked leaves and unstalked (= sessile) acorns (see Figure 49), unlike the oak of southern Britain (the pedunculate oak (*Quercus robur*)), which has unstalked, lobed leaves and long-stalked (= pedunculate) acorns. Pedunculate oaks were planted in parks in our area and they hybridise with sessile oaks. Although most trees can be identified as either sessile or pedunculate, intermediates are widespread. The oak was the most important tree of local coppice woods, providing the most sought after timber from the standards, and bark for tanning from both the standards and the underwood. The underwood was also used in coopers' work, basketwork and cleft paling making. Today oak is equally highly valued by conservationists because it supports over 250 species of insects which in turn attract a great variety of insectivorous birds.

It has already been pointed out that most local woods are on sloping ground, usually valley

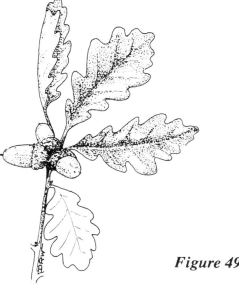

Figure 49. Sessile oak.

sides. On the higher slopes, where soils are shallow and nutrients have been washed out, rowan (mountain ash (*Sorbus aucuparia*)) grows among the generally small oaks. The rowan was long thought to have magical properties and its local name was **witchin** or **wiggin** (bewitched). Sidney Oldall Addy wrote in his *Sheffield Glossary* in 1888 that within living memory the people of Bradfield liked to have their bowls and spoons made from rowan because it was believed it gave protection from witchcraft. Birch, of which there are two native species, silver birch (*Betula pendula*) and downy birch (*Betula pubescens*), grows among the oaks and rowans on the upper slopes.

On the lower slopes where the soils are deeper and richer, the oak trees are taller and grow mixed with ash and wych elm. At the streamside at the bottom of the slope where waterlogging occurs alders and willows become common. Other less common native trees found amongst the more widely distributed oaks, rowans, birches, ashes, wych elms, alders and willows are crab apples, maples and wild cherries.

Beneath the tree canopy is a shrub layer composed of holly, hazel, hawthorn, elder, dog rose and guelder rose.

One of the most obvious differences between semi-natural ancient woods and plantations is that the distribution of trees and shrubs in ancient woods changes rapidly in response to soil conditions. An old wood is full of surprises as one tree species suddenly disappears and another takes its place, only to be replaced within a short distance by another. Uneven groupings and inexplicable changes in old woods are replaced in plantations by regularity and monotony.

However, it should be remembered that none of our local woods is made up only of native trees and shrubs. Deliberate planting of broadleaved and coniferous trees and invasion from adjoining land by vigorous species such as the sycamore have changed them greatly. Figure 50 shows in diagrammatic form the same wood as it might have looked (A) in 1650, (B) in 1890, and (C) at the beginning of the 1980s. In 1650 the wood is a coppice with standards with only native trees and shrubs. The main standards are oak, ash and alder. The underwood is mixed and there is a pollarded rowan on the upper boundary. By 1890 the wood has undergone a significant change. Coppicing is in decline and the wood is being converted to a mixed plantation by singling the coppice and planting in the gaps where timber trees have been removed. Conifers have been introduced to produce a crop to be harvested within 30-50 years, and hornbeams, chestnuts and beeches have been planted for ornament and for timber. By 1980 the wood has changed character once again. It now belongs to the City Council and is no longer worked as a commercial wood. It is full of trees of roughly the same age. The majority are mature or over mature and form a dense canopy. This results in relatively little light reaching the woodland floor and consequently there is only a sparse shrub layer, a totally different situation from the one in 1650 when the felling of timber and the cutting of coppice was a regular activity. Other obvious differences between the mid-seventeenth and late-twentieth century wood are the presence in the latter of decaying trees, a wider variety of species including invasive sycamore, and dead and dying elms affected by Dutch elm disease.

A-1650

B-1890

C-1980

Key:

pollard

young tree

recently felled coppice

coppice

over-mature tree

standard

tree singled from coppice stool

neglected coppice

shrub

dead tree

species

✱ ✱✱ rowan

‖‖‖‖ oak

═══ ash

wych elm

alder

birch

holly

hazel

hawthorn

conifer

beech

hornbeam

sycamore

sweet chestnut

DRW

Figure 50. Diagrammatic representation of a wood in the Sheffield area in 1650, 1890, and 1980.

69

Woodland herbs, grasses, woodrushes and sedges

One of the most striking features of ancient woods, and one which distinguishes them from recently established woods and plantations, is the rich and varied ground flora. One of the greatest delights of visiting woods like Ecclesall is to see the shafts of sunlight on carpets of wood anemones in April and bluebells in May. A walk through a coniferous plantation gives no such pleasure. It is dark and the ground is covered only in needles.

Ecologists believe that certain flowers (herbs), grasses, sedges and woodrushes are either restricted to or are rarely found outside ancient woods. This belief is based on the notion that the slowest colonisers, particularly those that usually spread vegetatively rather than by seed, will only be found in undisturbed woodland sites and long-established secondary woods. In our area one of the difficulties encountered in trying to apply this idea is that many of our relatively new woodlands are surrounded by old hedges which are themselves remnants of ancient woodland. **Ancient woodland botanical indicator species**, therefore, can spread relatively quickly into the recently established woodlands.

These ideas can be illustrated by looking at an ancient wood and two plantations at Tankersley. Figure 51 shows the presence or absence of ancient woodland indicators on the three sites as revealed by surveys carried out in the Spring and Summer of 1982 and 1983. Thorncliffe Wood is a known ancient wood, although it has been much disturbed by mining activity. Newbiggin Plantation, which is adjacent to Thorncliffe Wood, was established between 1810 and 1820 to

A. Species with a very strong affinity for ancient woods	Thorncliffe Wood	Newbiggin Plantation	Bell Ground Wood
Wood Anemone	*		
Yellow Archangel	*		
Sweet Woodruff	*		
Wood Melick	*	*	
Wood Millet	*	*	
Wood Sorrel	*		
B. Species with a moderately strong affininty for ancient woods			
Ramsons	*	*	
Bluebell	*	*	
Wild Strawberry	*		
Dog's Mercury	*	*	
Greater Stitchwort	*		
Common Violet	*		*
Total	12	5	1

Figure 51. Ancient woodland indicators on three sites at Tankersley.

cover ironstone and coal workings. Bell Ground Wood was established in the 1860s on an area of bell pits. Thorncliffe Wood is still predominantly an oak wood. Newbiggin Plantation is a mixed wood of oak, ash, wych elm, beech, sweet chestnut and sycamore. Bell Ground is basically a beech wood. The greatest contrast in Figure 51 is between Thorncliffe Wood and Bell Ground Plantation. Thorncliffe is a beautiful bluebell wood and there are also large drifts of wood anemone and yellow archangel. Altogether it has 12 species of flowers and grasses that are usually reckoned to be characteristic of ancient woods in this area. In contrast, Bell Ground Plantation has none. Bell Ground was formerly in an area of walled paddocks in Tankersley Park, which would have been heavily grazed for centuries and there were no old hedges in the near vicinity from which flowers and grasses could spread into the new plantation. No doubt its management as a beech wood with its very dense canopy also contributes to the sparseness of its ground vegetation. Newbiggin Plantation, by contrast, lies next to an ancient wood and the trees were planted in an area of small irregular fields whose hedges were remnants of ancient woodland. It was much easier, therefore, for slow colonisers to spread into Newbiggin Plantation than into Bell Ground.

A list of flowers, grasses, sedges and woodrushes believed to be strongly associated with ancient woodland in South Yorkshire is given in Figure 53 . Try it out in your local wood. If there are substantial numbers (say more than ten) of indicator species, and the wood appears to be ancient from historical and landscape evidence then all the factors taken together prove conclusively that the wood is ancient. However, if documentary and landscape evidence suggests a site is not ancient, the occurrence of a few indicator species cannot be taken to mean that it really is an ancient wood. Whatever the outcome, identifying and listing the flowers, grasses, sedges and woodrushes in your local wood adds to the enjoyment of walking there.

Woodland plants, whether or not they are indicators of ancient woods, are adapted to the varied and changing conditions in woods. Grasses and sedges take advantage of woodland glades,

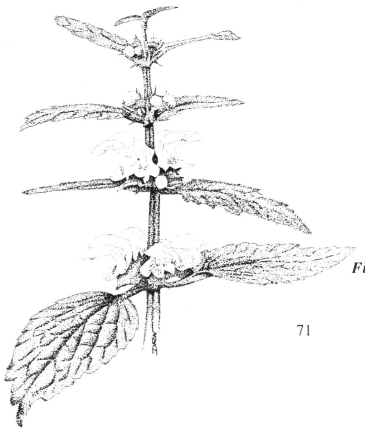

Figure 52. Yellow archangel, a strong indicator of ancient woodland.

71

rides, ditches and banks. Some flowering plants, called **pre-vernal** (before Spring), come into flower before the trees come into leaf. Wood anemone, dog's mercury, and primrose come into this category. Another group of plants, including common cow-wheat, toothwort and some orchids, live partly off food obtained from decomposing litter or the roots of other plants.

One of the greatest pleasures of visiting a coppice wood is to see the explosion of flowering plants following the cutting of the coppice. In the first summer after the cutting of the underwood to ground level, the ground vegetation makes vigorous growth in the intense sunlight, and in the succeeding few springs and summers there are spectacular carpets of colour until the rapidly growing coppice and coppicing 'weeds' such as thistle, rush and willowherb reduce the sunlight reaching the woodland floor and suppress the ground vegetation. Local woods that have been recently managed such as Bowden Housteads and Holmesfield Park can be expected to have increased displays of spring flowers for the next few years.

HERBS

No.	E	R	W	VS	Name
1				VS	Barren strawberry
2					Bluebell
3					Broad helleborine
4					Bugle
5				VS	Bush vetch
6					Common cow wheat
7				VS	Common St John's wort
8					Dog's mercury
9					Early purple orchid
10					Golden saxifrage
11					Greater stitchwort
12	E	R			Green hellebore
13					Hairy St John's wort
14	E			VS	Lily-of-the-valley
15	E			VS	Nettle-leaved bellflower
16					Pale wood violet
17					Pignut
18	E				Primrose
19					Ramsons
20					Sanicle
21					Slender St John's wort
22					Square stemmed St John's wort
23				VS	Sweet woodruff
24					Toothwort
25					Trailing St John's wort
26					Water avens
27					Wild strawberry
28				VS	Wood anemone
29					Wood horsetail
30				VS	Wood sorrel
31					Wood speedwell
32				VS	Yellow archangel
33				VS	Yellow pimpernel

GRASSES, SEDGES AND WOODRUSHES

No.	E	R	W	VS	Name
34				VS	Greater woodrush
35				VS	Hairy woodrush
36		R			Pale sedge
37		R		VS	Pendulous sedge
38	E	R			Purple small reed
39				VS	Remote sedge
40		R			Wood barley
41				VS	Wood melick
42				VS	Wood millet

SHRUBS AND TREES

No.	E	R	W	VS	Name
43					Field maple
44		R		VS	Midland hawthorn
45	E	R		VS	Wild service tree
46			W		Sessile oak
47	E	R		VS	Small-leaved lime
48	E	R			Spindle tree

Key

E found in east only, especially on limestone
W found predominantly in west and central areas in gritstone and coal measure country
R rare
VS very strongly associated with ancient woodland, rarely occurring elsewhere unless introduced or indicating recently cleared woodland

Figure 53. Ancient woodland botanical indicators in South Yorkshire.

PART 5: THE FUTURE OF SHEFFIELD'S WOODS

For almost a century most of Sheffield's ancient broadleaved woods, including those in private as well as public ownership, have been neglected and unmanaged except where dead or dying trees have been judged to be a danger to the public. After having survived for hundreds, and in many cases for thousands, of years there is a real danger that our woodland heritage will be squandered. Our ancestors quite deliberately protected the woods by actively managing them; the twentieth century attitude until lately in urban areas seems to have been, at best, to let them take care of themselves, and at worst, to abuse them unmercifully.

The City Council approved a Woodland Policy in 1987. Its primary aim is to ensure the protection and perpetuation of woodlands within the city and to realise their potential in as many ways as possible. The policy seeks to maintain the ancient woods in a healthy state, to protect, conserve and encourage their rich flora and fauna, and to preserve their important historical and archaeological value. In all this the public will be encouraged to play a full part by expressing their views, becoming involved in management, and monitoring effects and consequences. This policy is largely enshrined in the city's *Nature Conservation Strategy* document published in 1991.

At the time of writing the first edition of this book in late 1988 the Woodland Policy was already being implemented in Bowden Housteads Wood. This major management project in a badly neglected ancient wood, was funded jointly by the City Council and the Countryside Commission. The main operation was thinning, to provide more space for the native trees to develop, and to help diversify the woodland by encouraging the regeneration of the shrub layer and the flowering of the ground flora. The thinning was irregular and several glades were being created.

The project involved a major public relations campaign. Before the commencement of operations public meetings were held, and guided walks around the wood were undertaken. 400 letters were posted to local residents about the project, notices were posted up in and around the wood about what was about to be done and why, news items appeared in the local press and a broadcast was made on local radio. One important aspect of this campaign was to reassure local residents that felling trees did not mean the destruction of a well-loved wood. The point was made that the sound of a chain saw should be taken to be a sign of good woodland management practice not council vandalism.

This project was a major new departure in woodland management in the city. It was an 'active' rather than a 'care and maintenance' approach, and it was sympathetic both to the origins and history of the wood and to the local residents who are its users. When visited most recently in May of 1993, the wood was much improved compared to its character in the mid 1980s. The woodland has a more open aspect, there has been widespread regeneration of trees

73

and shrubs, the ground is no longer bare in large areas, and the glades that have been created add a new dimension to the woodland environment. Since the late 1980s woodland management has been extended to other sites and the last two winters has seen management activity in Roe Wood and Woolley Wood.

Good woodland management, however, is not a one-off operation; it is continuous and long term. It is also costly. What has taken place at Bowden Housteads Wood, Roe Wood and Woolley Wood is just a beginning there. Further management at short intervals over a long period will be necessary in order to achieve and maintain the sought-after uneven structure and the beauty and interest that it brings in its train. Can the City Council afford to repeat the treatment in the other 47 woodlands for which it is responsible? Can it afford not to? That is the challenge.

Figure 54. Active woodland management: glade creation in Bowden Housteads Wood.

REFERENCES AND FURTHER READING

Documents in Archive Collections

The main sources of primary documentary evidence have been the important collections held in Sheffield Record Office (formerly the Archives Division of Sheffield City Libraries). Particular use has been made of material in three collections:

the records of the Beauchief Estate : the Beauchief Muniments;

the records of the Duke of Norfolk's Estates: the Arundel Castle Manuscripts;

the records of the Fitzwilliam Wentworth Estate: the Wentworth Woodhouse Muniments.

Books and Articles

Colebourn, P and Gibbons, B (1987), *Britain's Natural Heritage - reading our countryside's past,* Blandford Press.

Edlin, H L (1949), *Woodland Crafts in Britain,* Batsford.

Evelyn, J (1706 edition), *Sylva or a Discourse of Forest-Trees.*

Jones, M (1984), 'Woodland Origins in a South Yorkshire Parish', *The Local Historian,* 16, pp. 78-83.

Jones, M & Jones, J L (1985) 'Traditional Woodland Management in the Sheffield region: An introductory survey', *Transactions of the Hunter Archaeological Society,* 13, pp. 1-9.

Jones, M (1986), 'Ancient woods in the Sheffield area: The documentary evidence', *Sorby Record,* 24, pp. 7-18.

Jones, M (1987), 'Trespassers will be prosecuted: Coppice wood offenders in the Sheffield area in the medieval and post-medieval period', *Old West Riding,* 7, No 1, pp. 9-12.

Linnard, W (1982), *Welsh Woods and Forests,* National Museum of Wales.

Marren, P (1990), *Woodland Heritage,* David & Charles.

NCC, (1990), *Coppiced Woodlands: their management for wildlife.*

Peterken, G (1981), *Woodland Conservation and Management,* Chapman & Hall.

Rackham, O (1976, revised edition 1992) *Trees and Woodland in the British Landscape,* Dent.

Rackham, O (1980), *Ancient Woodland,* Arnold.

Rackham, O (1986), *The History of the Countryside,* Dent.

Rackham, O (1986), *The Woodlands of South East Essex,* Rochford District Council.

Ronksley, J G (Ed), (1908), John Harrison's (1637) *Exact & Perfect Survey & View of the Manor of Sheffield.*

Scurfield, G (1986), 'Seventeenth Century Sheffield and Environs', *Yorkshire Archaeological Journal,* 58, pp. 147-171.

Spray, M and Smith, D J (1977), 'The Rise and Fall of Holly in the Sheffield Region', *Transactions of the Hunter Archaeological Society,* 10, pp. 239-251.

Watkins, C (1990), *Woodland Management and Conservation,* David & Charles.

INDEX